John Bull's Adventures
in the Fiscal Wonderland

John Bull's Adventures in the Fiscal Wonderland

An economic parody based on
Lewis Carroll's Wonderland

by Charles Geake &
Francis Carruthers Gould

ILLUSTRATED BY
FRANCIS CARRUTHERS GOULD

2010

Published by Evertype, Cnoc Sceichín, Leac an Anfa, Cathair na Mart, Co. Mhaigh Eo, Éire. *www.evertype.com*.

This edition © 2010 Michael Everson.

First edition London: Methuen & Co., 1904.

All rights reserved. No part of this publication may be reproduced, stored in a retrieval system, or transmitted, in any form or by any means, electronic, mechanical, photocopying, recording, or otherwise, without the prior permission in writing of the Publisher, or as expressly permitted by law, or under terms agreed with the appropriate reprographics rights organization.

A catalogue record for this book is available from the British Library.

ISBN-10 1-904808-51-4
ISBN-13 978-1-904808-51-0

Typeset in De Vinne Text, Mona Lisa, ENGRAVERS' ROMAN, and *Liberty* by Michael Everson.

Illustrations: Francis Carruthers Gould, 1904.

Cover: Michael Everson.

Printed by LightningSource.

Foreword

John Bull is the personification of Great Britain (or at least of England). He was first created in 1712 by John Arbuthnot, and eventually became a common sight in British editorial cartoons of the 19th and early 20th centuries. John is a sort of British Everyman, endowed with common sense and good intentions, who likes a pint of beer. In his trip to the Fiscal Wonderland, John's frustrations with the bewildering nonsensicality of economic politics are made apparent by the author and illustrator.

Charles Geake (1867–1919) was, from 1892 to 1918, the head of the Liberal Publication Department, which had been established in 1887 by the National Liberal Federation (a union of all English and Welsh (but not Scottish) Liberal Associations), and the Liberal Central Association (an organization which had been founded in 1874 to facilitate Liberal Party communication throughout United Kingdom.

Francis Carruthers Gould (1844–1925) was a political cartoonist and caricaturist who contributed to the *Pall Mall Gazette* until he joined the *Westminster Gazette* when it was founded. He later became an assistant editor for that publication. Before he illustrated *John Bull's Adventures in the Fiscal*

Wonderland in 1904, Gould had already done the illustrations for Saki's *Westminster Alice* in a series of publications from 1900 to 1902.

More than a century on, it is not always easy to identify the people caricatured by Gould. Still more arduous would be to attempt to explain the jokes and allusions by made by Geake—that would be material for an academic thesis. Nevertheless I can supply a few biographical summaries and photos to assist the reader to put the cartoon parodies into context and guide the reader who wishes to pursue an interest in any of these characters, or in the particulars of Tariff Reform, Free Trade, the Free Food League, etc.

Balfour Clock, Humpy Dumpy, March Hare: Arthur Balfour (1848–1930) was Prime Minister of the United Kingdom from 1902 to 1905. When Lord Salisbury resigned as Prime Minister in 1902 Balfour succeeded him. The beginning of Balfour's premiership thus coincided both with the end of the South African War and with the Coronation of Edward VII.

Chaplin Parakeet, the Chaplin: Henry Chaplin, 1st Viscount Chaplin (1840–1923) was a British landowner, racehorse owner and Conservative Party politician who sat in the House of Commons from 1868 until 1916 when he was raised to the peerage.

Vincent Parakeet, White Knight of Sheffield: Colonel Sir Charles Edward Howard Vincent (1849–1908), known as Howard Vincent or C.E. Howard Vincent, was a soldier, barrister and senior official in the Metropolitan Police. He sat as Conservative MP for Sheffield from 1885 to 1908.

The White Rabbit: Jesse Collings (1831–1920) was Mayor of Birmingham, a Liberal (later Liberal Unionist), and MP for Birmingham Bordesley from 1886 to 1918. He was best known in the UK as an advocate of educational and land reform; his slogan for this "Three Acres and a Cow" became the battle cry of the fight against rural poverty.

Hugha (the Anglo-Saxon Messenger): Hugh Richard Heathcote Gascoyne-Cecil, 1st Baron Quickswood (1869–1956) was a Conservative Party politician, known as Lord Hugh Cecil before 1941. He formed the Free Food League in 1904.

The Prefferwense, the Missioner, Mad Hatter, Cheshire Cat, the Aged Man, Father Joseph, Knave of Hearts: Joseph Chamberlain (1836–1914) opposed the Free Trade consensus that had dominated British economics since the repeal of the Corn Laws in 1846, in favour of an "Imperial Preference" system instead, for the good of what he thought of as Britain's imperial destiny and the welfare of the working class.

The Messenger, Father Joseph's Son: Austen Chamberlain (1863–1937) was the second child and eldest son of Joseph Chamberlain, born in Birmingham. He served as MP for East Worcestershire from 1892 to 1914.

Red Knight: Sir John Eldon Gorst (1835–1916) was MP for Cambridge University from 1892 to 1906. He served as Vice-President of the Committee on Education between 1895 and 1902.

Tweedle-R.: Archibald Philip Primrose, 5th Earl of Rosebery (1847–1929) was a Liberal statesman. He served as Foreign Secretary from 1892 to 1894 and as Prime Minister from 1894 to 1895. His enthusiasm for the Empire and his opposition to Home Rule for Ireland exacerbated divisions in the Liberal Party.

Twee-C.-B.: Sir Henry Campbell-Bannerman (1836–1908) became leader of the Liberals in the House of Commons in 1898. The Boer War (1899–1902) had split the Liberal party into Imperialist and Pro-Boer camps and the party was defeated in the "khaki election" of 1900.

Dormouse: Spencer Compton Cavendish, 8th Duke of Devonshire (1833–1908) known from 1858 to 1891, while heir to the Dukedom, as Marquess of Hartington. He joined Salisbury's third government in 1895 as Lord President of the Council, and resigned from Balfour's government in 1903, and from the Liberal Unionist Association the following spring, in protest at Joseph Chamberlain's Tariff Reform scheme.

Chanclerpillar: Hardinge Stanley Giffard (1823–1921) was the 1st Earl of Halsbury from 1898 to 1921. He was a barrister, politician and government minister who who was Lord Chancellor for three separate periods.

St Augustine Birrell: Augustine Birrell (1850–1933), barrister and author, was MP for Bristol North from 1906 to 1918.

Sunny Jim (of Hereford): Henry James, 1st Baron James of Hereford (1828–1911) served as Chancellor of the Duchy of Lancaster from 1895 to 1902 in the Unionist ministries of Lord Salisbury and Arthur Balfour.

Leg of Mutton: Richard Seddon (1845–1906) served as Prime Minister of New Zealand from 1893 to 1906. He had been a strong supporter of the Second Boer War and of preferential trade between British colonies, and believed that New Zealand should play a major role in the Pacific Islands as a "Britain of the South".

I think it is likely that the "Ritchie, Georgie, and Burlie" in the Dormouse's story are Charles Thomson Ritchie, 1st Baron Ritchie of Dundee (1838–1906), Lord George Francis Hamilton (1845– 1927), and Alexander Hugh Bruce, 6th Lord Balfour of Burleigh (1849–1921), all of whom resigned their posts in 1903 and were, in opposition to Joseph Chamberlain, advocates of Free Trade.

I hope I have identified the players correctly: I am really no expert in early twentieth-century British politics. Not that I, or you, need to be to enjoy this book. The story's parody of Lewis Carroll's *Wonderland* books is still relevant and amusing even today. Today's bankers and politicians seem not to have learned much from history. Regrettable as that is, at least Charles Geake and Francis Carruthers Gould can still make us laugh about it!

Michael Everson
Westport 2010

Preface to the 1904 edition

Our first word must be one of our sincere and appreciative acknowledgments to the Writer and Illustrator of the incomparable Alice Books—to Lewis Carroll, the one man who, if he had only been alive, could have made head or tail of Mr Chamberlain's figures, and to Sir John Tenniel, happily still in our midst, even though each succeeding Wednesday no longer brings with it an example of his genius.

It will be noticed that in the Fiscal Wonderland one actor has to sustain more than one of the characters of the Alice *dramatis personæ*. Mr Balfour is not only Humpy Dumpy, but also the March Hare; Mr Chamberlain is at once the Mad Hatter, the Cheshire Cat, and the Knave of the Trial. For this we make no apology, since one man in his time plays many parts, and in this fiscal controversy the time has been as short as the parts have been varied.

The Hatter's riddle (on page 50) as invented had not an answer any more than Lewis Carroll's original working model, but if an answer be desired, "Because neither can be obtained from Birmingham" would seem to have the merit of accuracy.

In writing and illustrating the Fiscal Wonderland, we do not pretend to having had no settled convictions. But whilst these have not been concealed, we venture to hope that none of the combatants in the Big Fight will find any cause of offence in this new version of the old stories, so much of which now seems only an intelligent anticipation of the present political situation.

C. G.
F. C. G.
January 1904

John Bull's Adventures in the Fiscal Wonderland

Contents

I. Through the Fiscal Glass *5*
II. The Fiscal Parade Ground *11*
III. The White Rabbit Explains *16*
IV. In Downing Street *21*
V. Humpy Dumpy *28*
VI. Tweedle-R. and Twee-C.-B. *38*
VII. The Mad Tea-Party *49*
VIII. "It's My Own Invention" *59*
IX. A Chanclerpillar gives Advice *73*
X. The Fiscal Tournament *81*
XI. Who Stole the Loaves? *97*
XII. John Bull's Evidence *105*

Chapter I

Through the Fiscal Glass

*J*ohn Bull sat in an easy-chair before the fireplace, but he was not by any means at ease. He had been reading the Blue Books of the War Commission, and his muttered comments as he turned over page after page of imbecilities branded in type were, like the covers, dark blue.

At last he flung the books down impatiently and threw himself back in his chair.

"Good heavens!" he exclaimed. "It's a wonder I even *muddled* through." And then he said bang words which were not very respectful to distinguished statesmen.

"Two hundred and fifty millions of money it has cost me!" he growled, and then he began to think what he could have done with all that money if he had not had to spend it.

All sorts of fanciful ideas crossed and recrossed his mind, until the tangled web made him drowsy, and the Blue Books faded into grey and vanished.

* * * *
 * * *
* * * *

He was aroused by a sound as of someone tapping at a window, and he opened his eyes and sat up. In front of him on the mantelshelf was a large pier-glass, with a clock in the middle of the shelf, and a stuffed parakeet under a glass case on either side. It was these objects that first attracted his attention, for they seemed to have changed in some magic way.

The face of the clock had turned into Mr Arthur Balfour's, and the heads of the two parakeets into those of Mr Henry Chaplin and Sir Howard Vincent. John rubbed his eyes and looked again. But there could be no doubt about it, for the Howard Vincent bird every now and then uttered the loud "Yah-yah" so familiar to the House of Commons, and the other had an eyeglass firmly fixed in the left eye.

There was something strange, too, about the pier-glass.

Across it sprawled large white figures in the form of a sum in addition—

$$2 + 2 = 3$$

THE FISCAL GLASS

The last figure certainly was 3 when John first noticed it, but presently it began to flicker, and then it appeared as 5, only to waver back again to 3. John watched this singular apparition with a sort of fascination, expecting each moment to see the correct result figured.

But no, the sum went on alternating between 3 and 5, with never a 4. John began to get annoyed.

"Hang it! Why ca'n't you get your sum right?" he exclaimed.

Of course the glass could not tell him, for fortunately mirrors ca'n't speak what they think.

But the clock began to strike, and it struck six; at least John tried to believe so, but the strokes seemed to him to have the sound of spoken words, and the words were—

No—set—tled—con—vic—tions.

And the parakeet on the left shouted "Yah-yah."

"No settled convictions!" John snorted contemptuously. "More like previous ones," and he glanced at the Blue Books.

The ridiculous addition sum went on working itself out wrong until John jumped up from his chair in a rage, picked up one of the books from the floor and flung it at the glass.

THE VINCENT PARAKEET

To his astonishment neither was there any smash of broken glass, nor did the book rebound: it just went noiselessly through and disappeared, apparently on the other side.

"There ca'n't be any glass there at all," he thought. "It must be an open space."

And yet the silly sum was there still.

"I must look into this business," John said to himself. "There's something weird going on."

So he looked round the room to find some way of clambering on to the mantelshelf. There was a pile of the *Encyclopædia Britannica* in one corner; he had bought them because it was the only way he could stop the dumping of circulars and samples into his letter-box.

THE CHAPLIN PARAKEET

"Wisdom whilst you wait," he said, with a smile. "I'm glad I got them, after all"; and he proceeded to pile the volumes one upon another. "I'm glad Moberly Bell ca'n't see me, or he'd use it as another advertisement," he thought, as he put on his hat—for he didn't know where he might be going—climbed the massive pile, and clambered on to the mantelshelf, to the manifest delight of the two parakeets under the glass shades. The pier-glass offered no resistance; like the one in Alice's adventures, it melted away in a bright silvery mist, and the next moment John was through on the other side.

Chapter II

The Fiscal Parade Ground

*J*ohn found himself in a large, square, level space enclosed by high walls, on which in gigantic letters the word "TARIFFS" was painted at intervals all round, and the tops of the walls were prickly with spikes and broken glass.

"It looks like a parade ground," John said. And so it evidently was, for in the middle of the square a battalion of very queer-looking soldiers was drawn up in close military formation.

No wonder they looked queer, for when John got a little nearer to them he found they were all large quartern loaves, drawn up as if to be drilled or inspected.

There was no band; only a very big drum, and that was being vigorously banged by a portly drummer, who marched backward and forward in front of the column, thumping the drum part of *"Rule Britannia"*. He wore a splendid, very early nineteenth-century uniform, with a tremendously tall shako, ornamented with a towering red, white, and blue plume.

JOHN BULL'S ADVENTURES IN THE FISCAL WONDERLAND

John was watching this strange parade, when he heard a stentorian "Shun!" from somewhere behind him, accompanied by a loud, metallic clanging and jangling noise.

"This must be the colonel or the inspecting officer," he thought.

He looked round and saw a sort of medieval White Knight, encased in a complete suit of tinplate armour which looked like riveted steel boiler-plates. He was jogging along towards the battalion in front of him on a white horse.

"I know that Knight; he comes from Sheffield," John remarked to himself.

There was nothing remarkable in the fact of this recognition, for the words "Made in Sheffield" were printed on his breastplate. From the pommel and the cantle of the saddle dangled a queer collection of things of various kinds, like samples of an ironmonger's stock.

"Shun!" shouted the Knight, as he pulled up his horse in front of the regiment of loaves. "Shun! Royal salute! Present arms!"

The big drummer changed his percussive tune to fit the National Anthem, and the Knight of Sheffield sat rigidly upright and stiff, with his right gauntlet raised to his helmet in salute.

But the quartern loaves never moved a crumb and stood stolidly still.

Then the drummer stopped his banging, and the Knight shouted, "*Pro—tection!*"

No sooner was the word out of his mouth than the loaves all began to shrink in a weird and mysterious way, as if they were in a haunted farm, getting smaller and smaller.

"As you were!" shouted the Knight excitedly.

Immediately the loaves resumed their normal size.

The Knight glared sternly at them.

"At the last sound of the word 'Protection' let me see every loaf pull itself together, throw its chest out, and look as big as possible.

"Now, then," he went on, "all together. *Pro—tection!*"

The loaves immediately began to dwindle again.

"As you were!" the Knight yelled, as he galumphed up and down. "This wo'n't do at all! Where's your discipline?

"Now then, once more," he shouted, when he had cooled down a little. "We'll try it again. I want you to look *bigger*, and not *smaller*, at the word of command.

"*Pro—tec—tion!*"

The loaves instantly began to shrink as before, and if the Knight of Sheffield had not had the presence of mind to shout "As you were!" just in time, they might have disappeared altogether.

The Knight was terribly angry, and presently he called up the big drummer, and the two talked together in a very excited manner.

When the conversation was ended the Knight turned to the regiment again and gave another word of command.

"The loaves will advance in price! Quick march!"

This time the loaves seemed as if they were going to obey, only instead of advancing at the quick step they started at the double and rushed straight towards the officer yelling "Yah-yah!" as they swept forward.

The Fiscal Parade Ground

"Halt! Halt!" the Knight shouted, but it was unheeded; the loaves had got thoroughly out of hand, and raced on in an irresistible wave.

The Knight gazed for a moment in speechless fury at the threatening mass of loaves, and then he hastily pulled his horse's head round and rode off clattering as fast as he could get his horse to lay its legs to the ground, all the ironmongery stock banging and clanging as they went.

"At any rate, I'm leading them!" he shouted to John Bull as he galloped past with the loaves yelling at his heels.

In a moment they were out of sight, leaving nothing behind but the big drummer, who had been knocked over in the charge, and who was sitting on the ground beside his broken drum, ruefully trying to get his battered shako into shape again.

Chapter III

The White Rabbit Explains

"Dear me!" said John Bull. "This is a curious sort of place; I wish I could find someone to tell me something about it." He had hardly wished when a little White Rabbit—at least, it looked like a White Rabbit—ran hastily past him.

"Hi! Hi!" John shouted. "Stop a minute. Could you kindly tell me—"

"Oh, please don't stop me!" cried the Rabbit, reluctantly turning round. "I'm so busy, and I'm late already." It took a large turnip watch out of its pocket and looked anxiously at it.

"What's the name of this queer place?" John asked.

"It's Tariff-land," said the White Rabbit, "and it isn't a queer place; it's very beautiful."

"But why has it got high walls all round?" John wanted to know.

"Oh!" said the White Rabbit eagerly, "That's Mr Joseph's own invention. It's to stop Dumping, you know."

"Dumping! What is that?" John asked.

"It's a lot of nasty, horrid foreigners trying to sell us things we want cheaper than we want to pay for them," said the White Rabbit.

"That's a funny idea," John remarked. "Your country wo'n't get very fat on that."

"Not get fat?" the White Rabbit exclaimed indignantly. "You should just see our Pigs; they're beautiful!"

"But what do they get fat on?" John asked.

"Maize!" said the White Rabbit proudly. "Mr Joseph lets the maize come in because the Pigs like it. There's one coming along now," he went on. "Isn't he splendid!" And the White Rabbit pointed to an extremely fat Pig waddling across the enclosure. "Would you like to hear the Pig sing?"

John Bull said he would, so the White Rabbit beckoned the Pig towards them. "Sing your '*Beautiful Maize*' song to this gentleman, will you, old fellow?"

The Pig sighed, and said he had a bad cold, but he would try. Then he struck an attitude and began to sing in a very throaty voice—

> *Beautiful Maize! that looks like gold,*
> *Loveliest cereal ever sold!*
> *Who wouldn't live on it all his days?*
> *Maize of the morning, beautiful Maize!*
> *Maize of the morning, beautiful Maize!*
> > *Beau–ootiful Ma–aize!*
> > *Beau–ootiful Ma–aize!*
> *Ma–aize of the mo-mo-morning,*
> > *Beautiful, beautiful Maize!*
>
> *Beautiful Bacon! who can feel*
> *Fond of mutton, beef, or veal?*
> *Who would not fly, the world forsaken,*
> *In order to save his beautiful Bacon?*
> *In order to save his beautiful Bacon?*
> > *Beau–ootiful Ma–aize!*
> > *Beau–ootiful Ba–acon!*
> *Ma–aize of the mo—mo—orning,*
> > *Beautiful, beauti–FUL BACON!*

When the Pig had finished, John thanked him politely, and the Pig waddled off.

"By-the-bye," said John to the White Rabbit, "you spoke of Mr Joseph just now. Do you mean Joe—"

The White Rabbit gave a little scream of horror, and stamped its feet angrily.

"You shut up!" it cried; "I wo'n't have it! You mustn't speak of him like that! If you were in Birmingham they would know how to treat you. My Mr Joseph is a Great Statesman!" and the White Rabbit glared very fiercely at John and shook its umbrella at him.

"I didn't mean to speak disrespectfully of him," John said. "Where is he now? Does he live here?"

"He's playing at a Cabinet card-party," the White Rabbit whispered mysteriously, "and I'm just going to see them shoot out of the chimney."

"What do you mean by going to see them shoot out of the chimney? Who are 'them'?"

"The others, of course," said the White Rabbit. "The ones Mr Joseph is playing against."

"Curiouser and curiouser," said John Bull to himself—just as Alice did once. "But what game are they playing? Whist?"

"It isn't exactly Whist," the White Rabbit replied. "It's a sort of Whist, but that's not the name of it."

"Is it Poker?" John asked.

"Yes, that's it," the White Rabbit said. "Red Hot Poker!"

"Rather a warm sort of game," John remarked. "But how do you know the others are going to get the worst of it?"

"Oh! They're sure to," the White Rabbit said eagerly. "Mr Joseph always shuffles the cards."

The White Rabbit looked at its watch again. "My goodness gracious!" it exclaimed. "You've kept me so long I sha'n't get there in time," and off it ran.

John hurried after it, for he didn't want to lose sight of his guide. And as he followed the White Rabbit it struck him that another strange thing had happened. He had actually shrunk in size until he was no bigger than the Rabbit.

"It's very awkward," he thought, "but I may as well see it through now I'm here."

Chapter IV

In Downing Street

The White Rabbit ran so fast that it was as much as John could do to keep it in sight, and at last, when it turned sharply round a corner, it disappeared altogether.

John followed as quickly as he could and found himself at the end of a narrow street. He looked up to see if he could find the name. It was Downing Street, but he noticed something else as well, for suddenly, out of a chimney a little way along the street, popped a large lizard, followed immediately by another.

There was a loud noise as if a crowd of people were watching sky-rockets let off, and shouts of "Here they come!"

The two lizards whizzed up very high in the air, and then curved gracefully away and disappeared.

Nothing was to be seen of the White Rabbit, but presently John heard the sounds of the running feet of a crowd and a tremendous shouting and screams of "He's out! He's loose!" A Lion and a Unicorn came running along, hotly arguing with each other. John Bull was not accustomed to see Lions and Unicorns in his daily walks, and he ought to have been startled; but there was something about this queer place which prevented him from being surprised at anything. So he called out to the two strange creatures—

"Excuse me, gentlemen, could you kindly tell me what it is that has got loose?"

"It's a very large, fierce, ramping, raging, tearing Dog!" said the Lion breathlessly.

"I beg your pardon," said the Unicorn scornfully. "Your eyesight must be defective. It was a gentleman in a large hat; the—er—Mad Hatter, in fact!"

The Lion snorted angrily. "I tell you it was a Dog!" he insisted.

The Unicorn sniffed contempt. "It was the Hatter!" he declared.

"But I made a sketch of it," exclaimed the Lion, "and here it is. Now is that a Hatter?" he asked, triumphantly flourishing a drawing of a Dog with an eyeglass and in violent action.

"Wait a moment," said the Unicorn. "Is that a Dog?" and he produced and waved before John's eyes a sketch of an unmistakable Mad Hatter.

"I'll fight you for a crown!" said the Lion, and then without another word the Lion and the Unicorn dropped their drawings, and began to rotate round each other in fighting attitudes.

A crowd quickly gathered, but John kept clear of the ring, for he thought it extremely silly to fight about the matter. But he could see in the middle of the crowd the rough head of the Lion and the horn of the Unicorn whirling round and round faster and faster. It struck John as another strange thing that he could see so well, for only a few minutes before he had been no bigger than the White Rabbit, so he came to the conclusion that he had acquired the property of sliding in and out like a telescope. And he had not been long in the Fiscal Wonderland before he found that this was exactly what had happened.

"They're at it again!" said a gentle voice by his side.

John looked round and saw a slim figure standing in a stained-glass, Anglo-Saxon attitude. "Pardon me," said John, "but your figure is familiar to me. Have I met you before?"

"Very likely," was the answer. "My name is Hugha, and I am an Anglo-Saxon messenger. Permit me to give you a tract," and he took a pamphlet out of a large bag which he carried on his left side, labelled "Free Food League", handed it to John, and hurried away round the nearest corner.

John took it, and saw at a glance that it was poetry of some kind, but it seemed to be printed in some strange characters. It began like this—

Prefferwensy

*'Twas maffig, and the brumming coves
Did cirk and cristle on the trade;
All mimsy were the quarternloaves,
And the tome balls outplude.*

John puzzled over it, but for a time could make nothing either of the language or the lettering.

In Downing Street

"It's an upside-down sort of a place," he muttered to himself "I'll try it that way."

It was a happy thought, for, after all, it was only printed upside down, and this was the poem:—

Prefferwensy

'Twas maffig, and the brummy coves
    Did cirk and cristle on the trade;
All mimsy were the quarternloaves,
    And the tome balfs outplade.

"Beware the Prefferwense, my son!
    The taxes that retaliate!
Beware the Joejoe bird and shun
    The jubious Seventydate!"

He took his Cobden club in hand,
    Long time the bunkome foe he sought,
So rested he by the Brumbrum tree,
    And stood awhile and thought.

And as in loafish thought he stood,
    The Prefferwense, with eye of flame,
Came piffling through the fiscey wood
    And shibbolled as it came.

One, two! And through the '72
    The Cobden club went snicker-snack!
He left it dead and with its head
    Went rollickeering back.

"And hast thou slain the Prefferwense?
    Come to my arms, my gladdish boy!
O dumpless day! Loaffooh! Loaffay!"
    He chortled in his joy.

'Twas maffig, and the brummy coves
    Did cirk and cristle on the trade;
All mimsy were the quarternloaves,
    And the tome balfs outplade.

"It's funny," he said when he had finished it, "but it's *rather* hard to understand. I seem to recognize some of it, and it's evident that something dangerous has got loose and has to be knocked on the head."

He turned round to see if he could find anyone to explain the meaning of some of the words, but everybody had vanished.

"I'd better see if I can get back through that glass and into my armchair again," he said, and he walked away down the street the way he had come.

CHAPTER V

Humpy Dumpy

John Bull had not gone very far when he heard a voice hailing him. He looked round and saw a queer-looking figure perched on a wall. At first he thought it was an egg, but as he went nearer it grew larger and larger, and more and more human, and he saw that it had eyes and a nose and mouth.

"It must be Humpy Dumpy; it ca'n't be anybody else!" he said to himself.

Humpy Dumpy was sitting on the top of a high wall; such a narrow one that John wondered how he could keep his balance.

John couldn't help repeating to himself—

> *Humpy Dumpy sat on a wall;*
> *Humpy Dumpy had a great fall;*
> *All the King's horses and all the King's men*
> *Had considerable difficulty in putting Humpy Dumpy in*
>   *his place again.*

"That last line's too long!" said Humpy Dumpy crossly. "It isn't poetry."

"It mayn't be poetry," said John, "but it's a fact all the same."

"You're rude," said Humpy Dumpy. "I don't like your methods; they're so Cliffordish!"

"How did you get up there on that wall?" John asked, to change the conversation.

Humpy Dumpy looked puzzled. "I suppose I must have played on to it," he said.

"Then you're what they call bunkered," John remarked.

"No, I'm not," Humpy Dumpy replied indignantly.

"But you would be if you fell off," John said.

"Fall off!" Humpy Dumpy exclaimed, with a look of surprise. "Why, if ever I *did* fall off—which there's no chance of—but *if* I did—" Here he pursed up his lips and looked so solemn and mysterious that John could hardly help laughing. "*If* I did fall," he went on, "*Joe has promised me*—ah, you may turn pale, if you like! You didn't think I was going to say that, did you?—*Joe has promised me—with his very own mouth*—to—to—"

"To be loyal to you," John interrupted rather unwisely.

"Now I declare that's too bad!" Humpy Dumpy cried, breaking into a sudden passion. "You've been listening at Cabinet doors—and behind trees—and down chimneys—and peeping into envelopes—or you couldn't have known it!"

"I haven't, indeed!" John said soothingly. "It's all been in the papers."

"Ah well! *They* may put such things in the *papers*. *I* never read them," Humpy Dumpy said loftily. "Now take a good look at me," he went on. "I'm a Leader, and I mean to lead; maybe you'll never see such another, and to show you I'm not proud—you may buy my little book, price one shilling—but you mustn't on any account quote more than a thousand words from it," and he smiled sweetly as he leant forward (and as nearly as possible fell off the wall in doing so) and offered John the book.

"I don't want it," said John, "and even if I did, I shouldn't think of paying a shilling for it."

Humpy Dumpy looked pained.

"It's an imputation on my personal honour," he said.

"Nonsense!" said John.

"Your insularity is something shocking," said Humpy Dumpy very severely.

"Would you tell me, please," said John, "what that means?"

"You'd have found it in my little book if you had only bought it, as I wanted you to, but I don't mind telling you. I meant by 'insularity' that if you go on as you are doing now, and don't do as other people do, you'll do for yourself."

"You seem very clever at using words, sir," said John. "Perhaps you could help me to understand what some mean. Would you kindly tell me the meaning of the poem 'Prefferwensy'?"

"Let's hear it," said Humpy Dumpy. "I've never found a poem yet I couldn't understand."

That sounded promising, so John repeated the first verse:—

'Twas maffig, and the brummy coves
    Did cirk and cristle on the trade;
All mimsy were the quarternloaves,
    And the tome balfs outplade.

"That'll do for a start," Humpy Dumpy interrupted. "There are plenty of hard words to begin on. '*Maffig*' means eleven o'clock at night—the time when you *maffick* and tickle each other with teasers and peacock's feathers."

"That's quite plain," said John. "And *'brummy'*?"

"Well, *'brummy'* means 'brum and rummy'. 'Brum' is just short for Brummagem. It's a portmanteau word—the sort that Lewis Carroll invented."

"I see it now," said John thoughtfully. "And what are *'coves'*?"

"Well, *'coves'* are something like dodgers—they're something like Tories—and they're something like turncoats."

"They must be very curious creatures."

"So they are," said Humpy Dumpy; "also they make their nests in Government offices; also they live on orchids."

"And what are to *'cirk'* and to *'cristle'*?"

"To *'cirk'* is to go round and round in a circle till you don't know where you are. To *'cristle'* is to make crystals like a wanklyn."

"And the *'trade'*?"

"Oh, the less said about the *'trade'* the better," said Humpy Dumpy.

"Isn't it a thing with a yoke that you feel?" said John, moved to make a suggestion.

"Of course it is. Well, then, *'mimsy'*, as everybody knows, means 'flimsy and miserable'. And a *'quarternloave'* is a comic-looking thing, something like a double crinoline—with a big dimple on top."

"And then *'tome balfs'*?" said John. "Though that sounds dreadfully difficult."

"It is, rather. A *'balf'* is a sort of child, rather like me; but *'tome'* is a real puzzler. I think it must be 'not at home'—meaning that they were unsettled down in their convictions, you know."

"Yes, I think I do know," said John, looking as if he remembered. "And what does *'outplade'* mean?"

"Well, *'outplaying'* means playing out and out and never getting home. However, you'll see it done maybe—down on the links yonder—and when you've once seen it you'll be *quite* content. Wherever did you get hold of all that hard stuff?"

"I read that in a book," said John. "But I heard some poetry recited that was a good deal easier."

"As to poetry, you know," said Humpy Dumpy, "*I* can repeat poetry if I'm really put to it—"

"Oh, I shouldn't like to put you to anything," said John, though he felt that he was in for another recitation.

"The piece I am going to repeat," he went on, "was written entirely for my own amusement."

John thought that in that case it was very hard lines he should have to listen to it, but rather than offend Humpy Dumpy, he sat down and said, "Thank you," looking a little apprehensive.

> *In Downing Street, when it is night,*
> *I troll this song for sheer delight.*

"I don't really troll it," he explained, "because of the policemen."

> *In Scotland when the links are green,*
> *I'll try and tell you what I mean.*

"Thank you very much," said John, "but you ought to know my handicap is thirty-six."

"All the better," said Humpy Dumpy, as he proceeded.

> *In Parliament, next Walter Long,*
> *I sometimes sing this simple song.*
>
> *In autumn, when we're out of town,*
> *Take pen and ink and write this down.*

"Of course, if you sing it in Parliament," said John, "I can read it in the papers."

"Oh, I never read the papers," said Humpy Dumpy rather testily. "They're not sensible, and they put me out."

> *I only sent him private word,*
> *"I think so, though it seems absurd."*
>
> *I sent a summons to the rest,*
> *Their clothes were just their second best.*
>
> *They sat around and talked away,*
> *It seemed the best part of a day.*

"It seems to be quite simple so far," said John, rather pleased at understanding so much.

"Oh, it gets harder all right later on," Humpy Dumpy replied.

> *He told them once, he told them twice,*
> *They would not listen to advice.*
>
> *The only thing I dared to say*
> *Was "Better let him have his way."*
>
> *They only answered, with a grin,*
> *"Why, what a temper you are in!"*
>
> *He said to them, he said it plain,*
> *"Then I shall not be here again."*
>
> *He said it very loud and clear,*
> *He whispered it in Austen's ear.*

Humpy Dumpy

I felt the letter large and new,
Fit for the deed I had to do.

My heart went thumps my heart went hop,
He signalled me to let it stop.

So no one knew of it because
I left the letter where it was.

Then someone came to me and said,
"Against this game we four are dead."

I said, "Just see the other three,
And bring their answers back to me."

Humpy Dumpy spoke in a whisper as he repeated the verse, and John thought, with a shudder, "I wouldn't have been the messenger for anything."

> *He brought them, I did not forget*
> *To send them on to the "Gazette".*
>
> *I showed the letter large and new,*
> *It did the trick I wanted to.*
>
> *I spoke at length, and all agreed*
> *That only I was fit to lead.*
>
> *But he was riled (Dukes often are)*
> *And said, "You shouldn't go so far."*
>
> *And he (Dukes often are) was riled;*
> *He said, "I thought you were a* CHILD—"
>
> *He took a form from off the shelf,*
> *And went and wired it off himself.*
>
> *And when I found he'd bolted too,*
> *I made no end of a to-do.*
>
> *And he who wrote the letter said,*
> *"If* ONLY *I had known instead—"*

There was a long, painful pause.

"Is that all?" John timidly asked.

"That's all for the present," said Humpy Dumpy. "Good-bye."

This was rather sudden, but John thought it would be rude to stay after this strong hint. So having thanked Humpy

Dumpy for all the poetry, John took the only path there seemed to be, and wondered what he should do when the roads divided. But whenever they did there were sure to be two finger-posts pointing the same way, one marked "TO TWEEDLE-R.'S TABERNACLE", and the other "TO THE TABERNACLE OF TWEE-C.-B."

"I do believe," John said at last, "that they must be living now in the same tabernacle. But from what they told me I never thought that possible."

Just as he said that he turned a corner, and there were two little men. This was all so sudden that John gave a start, but he pulled himself together, for he felt now that they must be—

Chapter VI

Tweedle-R. and Twee-C.B.

They were standing under a tree, with their arms lovingly entwined about each other's neck, and John Bull had no difficulty at all in knowing which was which, because one of them had "R." embroidered on his collar, and the other "C.-B."

They stood stock still, and John quite forgot, in the excitement of the moment, that they were alive. He was just looking to see whether the rest of their names was written at the backs of their collars, when all at once a voice came from the one marked "R."

"If you think we're enemies," he said, "you're not up to date, you know. The Education Act wasn't passed for nothing, nohow!"

"Contrariwise," added the one marked "C.-B.", "if you think we're friends, you ought to speak."

"I'm sure I'm very sorry," said John.

That, indeed, was all he could think of to say, for when he looked at the two little men the words of the old song kept running through his head like the paddle-wheel of a steamer, and he actually found himself saying them out loud—

> Tweedle-R., and Twee-C.-B.
> Were fighting, very nearly;
> For Twee-C.-B. said Tweedle-R.
> Had made his pitch play queerly.
>
> Just then they saw a grinning cat,
> As big as a beer barrel,
> Which frightened both the heroes that
> They swore no more to quarrel.

"I hear everything you're saying," said Tweedle-R., "and so it is, anyhow."

"Similarly," continued Twee-C.-B., "as it was, so it had to be; and as it might have been, it hadn't any need to be; but as it is, it is. That's logic."

John thought this was much too puzzling, so he thought he would ask them how they had made it up.

"Please," said John very politely, "everybody was *quite* certain you could never be friends any more."

"We couldn't," said Tweedle-R. "That was exactly what I said."

"But we are, you see," said Twee-C.-B. rather quickly and (so John thought) nervously.

"You *couldn't*, but you *are*," said John. "I'm afraid I don't understand."

"Well, you see," said Tweedle-R., "it's like this. If some morning at breakfast someone wanted you to go to bed and sleep, you'd say, 'I *couldn't*', but if they came and looked at you after supper they'd find you sleeping and say, 'You *are*'."

John thought this rather far-fetched, but he didn't say so; indeed he didn't say anything, for all at once Twee-C.-B., who seemed to have been turning something over in his mind, said, "All the same, I don't think you need have *thrown* the olive branch at me."

"I don't think you should have asked me the question," retorted Tweedle-R., taking away his arm from off Twee-C.-B.'s neck.

"You're too touchy," said Twee-C.-B., who by this time had also taken away his arm.

John was very frightened at this, because he was afraid that all the old trouble would begin over again. But suddenly they both put their arms round each other's neck again, looking very scared.

"The Cat," they said together in a frightened voice.

John followed the direction of their eyes, and there up in a tree was a large Cat grinning at them all.

No one said a word, and as they looked it vanished quite slowly, till nothing but the grin remained. At last even that went too.

"I hope you're not *very* much frightened?" said John by way of saying something.

"Nohow. And thank you for not running away," said Tweedle-R.

"Thank you *very* much," added Twee-C.-B. "You like poetry?"

"Ye—es," said John, "I like some kinds of poetry. But can you tell me which is my way out of the wood?"

"What shall I recite to him?" said Twee-C.-B., looking round to Tweedle-R., who stood there with great solemn eyes, neither paying any heed to John's questions.

"'*The Chaplin and the Missioner*' is the longest," Tweedle-R. replied.

Twee-C.-B. began instantly—

The sun was shining—

Here John made a last desperate attempt. "If it's more than four verses," he said, "would you tell me first which road—"
Twee-C.-B. only smiled and began again—

The sun was dumping on the sea,
    Dumping with all his might.
He did his best to rule the waves,
    And rule them nice and bright;
And this was odd, because it was
    The middle of the night.

The moon was shining sulkily,
    Because she thought the sun
Had really got no right to dump
    After the day was done.
"It's not legitimate," she said,
    "To come and spoil my fun."

The C. was cute as cute could be,
    The speeches dry as dry;
You could not see the reason, since
    There was no reason why:
No facts were flying overhead—
    There were no facts to fly.

The Chaplin and the Missioner
    Were walking glove in hand;
They wept like anything to see
    Such quantities of sand:
"If this were only tilled with wheat,"
    They said, "it WOULD be grand!"

Tweedle-R. and Twee-C.-B.

"If Seddon with a seven-bob tax
   Worked it for half a year,
Do you suppose," the Chaplin said,
   "That he could make bread dear?"
"I guess so," said the Missioner,
   And raised a British cheer.

"O Toilers, come and walk with us!"
   The Chaplin did beseech,
"A simple plan, a pleasant walk,
   A trampling on the Beach:
We cannot do with more than four
   To keep an eye on each."

The eldest Toiler looked at him,
   But never a word said he.
The eldest Toiler winked his eye
   And breathed a silent D,
Meaning to say he'd had enough
   Of such simplicity.

But four young Toilers hurried up,
    All eager for the plan;
They'd paid a guinea for their hats,
    Their clothes were spick and span—
And this was odd because, you know,
    Each was a working-man.

Four other Toilers followed them,
    And yet another four;
And thick and fast they came at last,
    And more and more and more—
So great a demonstration
    Was never seen before.

The Chaplin and the Missioner
    Walked on a mile or so,
And then they settled on a scheme
    Conveniently low:
And all the little Toilers stood
    And listened in a row.

"The time has come," the Chaplin said,
    "To talk of many things,
Of watches—wire—and Waltham clocks,
    Of pearlies—dolls—and rings,
And why you take it lying down,
    And whether trusts have wings."

Tweedle-R. and Twee-C.-B.

"But wait a bit," the Toilers cried,
    "Before we have our chat,
For listening is uncommon dry,
    And all of us are fat."
"No hurry," said the Missioner;
    They thanked him much for that.

"A tax on bread," the Chaplin said—
    "Two shillings, shall we say?
Mutton and beef and eggs and cheese
    Contribute in their way.
Now if you're ready, Toilers dear,
    You can begin to pay."

"The foreigner, not US!" they cried,
    Turning a little blue;
"After your pledge, to pay would be
    A dismal thing to do."
"The Empire's fine," the Chaplin said,
    "Do you admire the view?"

*"It was so kind of you to come,
    You looked so green and nice."
The Missioner said nothing but,
    "They're deaf to your advice;
I wish you would not perorate—
    I've had to stop you twice."*

*"It seems a shame," the Chaplin said,
    "To play them such a trick,
After we've led them on so far
    And talked to them so quick."
The Missioner said nothing but,
    "We've piled it on too thick."*

*"I beg of you," the Chaplin said,
    "Don't act contrariwise."
With hums and hahs he blurted out
    Words of the largest size,
Showing his pocket-handkerchief
    Before their wondering eyes.*

> *"O Toilers," said the Missioner,*
> *"You've had a pleasant run!*
> *Wo'n't you be giving me your votes?"*
> *But answer came there none—*
> *And this was scarcely odd, because*
> *They'd bolted, every one!*

"I like the Chaplin best," said John, "because, you see, he was a *little* sorry for the trick they played on the poor Toilers."

"It was his idea in the first place, though," said Twee-C.-B. "He'll be waiting for years and years and years for someone daring enough to play the trick."

"How shameful!" John said indignantly. "Then I like the Missioner best—if he was only persuaded into it by the Chaplin."

"But he wasn't," said Tweedle-R. "He wasn't the sort of person to be persuaded into anything he didn't want to do."

This seemed to make it a case of dishonours easy. After a little, John began, "Well, they were *both* very unpleasant characters—"

He had got thus far when all of a sudden Tweedle-R. and Twee-C.-B. took hold of each other's hands and took to their heels. John was puzzled at this, till he looked up, and there in the tree was the Cat once more.

John's first impulse was to run away too, but on second thoughts it seemed silly to be so frightened, so he thought he would speak to it.

"Saucy Puss—" he began timidly, as he did not know whether it was this breed of Cat; however, it only grinned, and did not seem offended "—would you tell me, please, where I ought to go from here?"

"It all depends," said the Cat, "on whether you're a Tariff Reformer."

"I think," said John, though he didn't see what the Cat was driving at, "that I'm a Free Trader."

"Then it would take Mr Seddon to say where you're sure to go," said the Cat.

John felt it would be dangerous to ask to have this explained, so he began on another tack. "What sort of people live about here?"

"In *that* direction," the Cat said, waving its right paw round, "lives a Hatter, and in *that* direction," waving the other, "lives a March Hare. Visit either you like, they're sure to be found together, and they're both mad."

"But I'd rather not visit either if they're both mad," said John.

"Oh, you ca'n't help that here!" said the Cat. "It's a mad world, you know—Shakespeare said so, you know, and he lived in *my* county. I'm mad—Ritchie made me mad. You're mad!"

"What makes you think I'm mad?" said John.

"You must be mad," said the Cat, "or you wouldn't continue to go about unprotected."

John knew there was some meaning in this, but he didn't know what it was, so saying "Good day, Puss," very politely, he walked off in the direction where the March Hare was said to live. In a very little while he came to what looked like a palace with a large tower with a clock in it. Policemen touched their hats to him, and the traffic stopped to let him get across the street. John felt sure that this must be the March Hare's house, but he was very disturbed at the thought that it might be mad. "Perhaps after all I ought to have gone to the Hatter's, though, to be sure, the Cat said I should find them both together."

CHAPTER VII

There was a table set out on a terrace in front of the House, and the March Hare and the Mad Hatter were having tea at it; a Dormouse was sitting between them fast asleep, quite unmindful of the conversation of the other two.

"How horrid for the Dormouse!" thought John Bull to himself. "Only, as it seems to be asleep, I suppose it doesn't understand what the other two are saying."

The table was an enormous one, but the three were all at one corner of it. "No trade! No trade!" cried the Hatter inconsequently when he saw John coming. "There's *plenty* of trade," said John indignantly, although he thought it all a curious kind of welcome and he sat down in a comfortable armchair at one end of the table.

"Have some jam?" said the March Hare, looking for approval to the Hatter.

John looked all round the table to see how many sorts of jam there were, but couldn't see any of any sort. "I don't see any jam," he said.

"There isn't any," said the March Hare.

John Bull's Adventures in the Fiscal Wonderland

"They're all making sugar!" shouted the Mad Hatter.

"Then it wasn't very polite of you to offer jam," said John, mightily offended.

"Oh! You needn't look for manners here," said the Dormouse, suddenly waking up, only to relapse at once into sleep.

"If you come to that," said the March Hare, "I should like to know who asked you to take the armchair?"

"I beg your pardon," said John, "but I thought it was meant for me."

"You're practically stagnant," said the Hatter. He had been studying John for some time, and said this with an air of great deliberation.

"You'd get on a good deal better," said John, "if you weren't so personal. But there, I suppose you ca'n't help it."

The Hatter put up his eyeglass and made as though he would hit back; but all he did was to *say*, "Why is a pearl button like an Old Age Pension?"

"Come, we shall have some sport now," thought John. "They told me that he was always asking conundrums, and they're quite right. I believe I could guess that," he added aloud.

"Do you mean that that isn't unanswerable?" said the March Hare.

"Well, if you must put it in that roundabout way, yes."

"Then you should say what you mean," the March Hare said, with all the air and mien of a leader.

"I always do," said John, feeling, however, considerably flustered. "At all events, I mean what I say—which is pretty much the same thing."

"Not a bit the same thing," said the Hatter. "You might as well say that 'I hit what I see' is the same as 'I see what I hit'."

"You might just as well say," added the March Hare, "that 'I think what I like' is the same thing as 'I like what I think'."

"You might just as well say," added the Dormouse, talking in his sleep, "that 'I know when I resign' is the same as 'I resign when I know'."

Here both the March Hare and the Hatter sat on the Dormouse, and the party sat silent for a little, whilst John thought over all he could remember about pearl buttons (which was not much) and Old Age Pensions (which was a good deal).

The Hatter was the first to speak. "What year is it?" he said, turning to John; he had taken his watch out of his pocket and was looking at it very thoughtfully, as if he were trying to find out where it was made.

John considered a little, and then said, "Well, not 1872."

"I told you cooking wouldn't suit the statistics," said the March Hare.

"I did the cooking myself," said the Hatter.

"Yes, but too many cooks spoil the argument," said the March Hare. "I always say right off what comes in my head first."

The Hatter kept on gloomily looking at the watch; then he pulled out the mainspring to see if it would tell the year any better; but all he did was to murmur sadly, "The sea voyage across the Atlantic didn't suit it; it ought to have been made at Prescot."

John had been looking at the watch with some curiosity. "What an odd sort of a watch!" he said. "All the years are marked on it, but the hands always point to 1872."

"Why shouldn't they?" said the Hatter rather crossly. "Doesn't *your* watch ever point to that year?"

"Of course it did," John replied very readily. "But it doesn't point to that year for such a long time together."

"Well, mine does," said the Hatter.

"Though any other year would do," the March Hare reminded the Hatter.

"Exactly what I said myself," he said.

John felt dreadfully puzzled. They seemed to be talking in quotations, though he didn't know where from. "I don't quite understand," he said as politely as he could.

"The Dormouse is asleep again," said the Hatter, and he poured a little hot tea upon its nose.

The Dormouse yawned impatiently, and said without opening its eyes, "Of course, of course; I told him he needn't post the letter unless he wanted to."

"Have you guessed the riddle yet?" the Hatter said, turning to John again.

"No; I give it up," John replied. "What's the answer?"

"That's exactly what I want to find out myself," said the Hatter.

"I was convinced I knew once," said the March Hare, "but now my convictions are so unsettled that I haven't the slightest idea."

"Don't you know any easy riddles that have got answers?" said John a little plaintively.

The Mad Tea-Party

"I know one," said the Hatter. "Why am I called a Whole Hogger?"

John smiled; it did seem such an easy one.

"Because," he said very hopefully, "you want to go it, I suppose."

"I knew he'd say that," said the March Hare triumphantly.

"Isn't it right?" said John gloomily.

"Of course not," said the Hatter. "The real answer is, 'Because I wo'n't tax bacon'."

"I know an easy riddle, too," said the March Hare. "What is a Little Englander?"

"That's a question, not a riddle," said John, who was getting tired of being trifled with.

"Well, anyhow, you don't know the answer," said the March Hare.

"What is it?" said John.

"Why, a person who thinks too much of England, of course," said the Hatter.

"You might let me answer my own riddles myself," said the March Hare rather peevishly.

John sighed deep and long. "I think you might spend the time of the House better," he said, "than in wasting it on foolish riddles."

"That's because you don't know Time," said the Hatter. "If you only know Time and keep on good terms with him you can do almost what you like with him. For instance, two or three years ago we just whispered to him the War was over, and in a twinkling it was time for a General Election!"

"That must be very convenient," said John, looking for once as if he knew all about what was being told him.

"We quarrelled last March," said the Hatter, "just before Ritchie made me and him mad, you know" (pointing with a long teaspoon to the March Hare). "It was at a great Pow-Wow in Downing Street, and I had to sing—

> *Dwindle, dwindle, British trade!*
> *By the foreigner betrayed!*

You know the song, perhaps?"

"I know something like it," said John.

"It goes on, you know," the Hatter continued, in this way—

> *With the tariff walls so high*
> *Down to zero point you fly.*
>   *Dwindle, dwindle—*

Here the Dormouse began to murmur, "*Dwindle, dwindle, dwindle, dwindle—*" and wouldn't stop till the March Hare gave it a sharp rap with a letter.

"Well, I'd hardly finished the first verse," said the Hatter, "when the whistle went and they all shouted 'Time! Time!'"

"He *must* have been cross," said John.

"And ever since then," the Hatter said mournfully, "he wo'n't do a thing I ask. It's always 1872 now."

The Hatter looked so worried that John thought it prudent to change the subject. "Why are so many tea-things put out here?" he asked.

"Well, you see," said the March Hare, "there used to be such a lot more to have tea."

"But the cups look as if they were used," said John.

"So they are," said the March Hare. "But it's always tea-time because it's always afternoon, and there's too much dirty linen to wash to worry over cups."

"Then you keep moving round, I suppose," said John.

"Suppose *we* change the subject," said the March Hare, who was getting very bored. "I vote the gentleman tells us a story."

"So do I," said the Hatter. "I'd tell one myself if I could. But I ca'n't, try how I will."

"Well, I *am* surprised," said John, plucking up courage to say so much.

"Don't be personal," said the Hatter. "We're waiting for your story."

"Please," said John, who was afraid he had offended the Hatter, "I don't know one."

"Then the Dormouse shall!" they both cried. "Wake up, my Harly," they cried, using its pet name and squeezing it on both sides at once.

The Dormouse slowly opened its eyes. "I wasn't asleep at all," he said. "I heard every word you fellows said."

"Tell us a story," said the March Hare.

"And be quick about it," said the Hatter, "or I shall have to hurry off to my Committee before you've done."

"Once upon a time there were three little brothers," the Dormouse began in a great hurry, "and their names were Ritchie, Georgie, and Burlie; and they lived at the bottom of a well—"

"What did they live on?" said John, who always liked hearing about good living.

"They lived on freefood," said the Dormouse, after pondering for a few seconds.

"They couldn't have done that, you know," said the Hatter. "It would have made them sick."

"That's just what they were," said the Dormouse. "*Very* sick."

John could make nothing at all out of it, but he said, "Why did they live at the bottom of a well?"

"Take some more tea," said the March Hare, with an air of intense settled conviction.

"It's the best Indian," said the Hatter proudly.

"Why, I didn't know you knew so much geography," said John.

"Who's arguing like a lawyer now?" said the Hatter triumphantly.

John did wish that they would not talk in inverted commas; so he helped himself to some tea and bread and butter—every slice of which had "Grown in Canada" stamped on it in red—and then turned to the Dormouse and repeated his question. "Why did they live at the bottom of a well?"

The Dormouse yawned two or three times and then said, "Because Truth lived there."

"There's no such thing," the Hatter shrieked, but the March Hare went "Sh! Sh!" and the Dormouse sulkily remarked, "If you ca'n't be civil I shall go to sleep again; I could easily."

"No, please go on," said John. So the Dormouse continued, "And so these three little brothers—they were learning to draw, you know—"

"What did they draw?" said John eagerly.

"Salaries," said the Hatter before the Dormouse had time to answer.

The Dormouse was so angry at being interrupted that he began to go to sleep, but before even he had time to get off the Hatter said, "I want a clean cup; let's move one place on."

They all moved on one place, but the Hatter was the only one who reaped any advantage from the change; and John was a good deal worse off, as the March Hare had covered the tablecloth with illegible notes and horrible drawings of imaginary islands.

"They were learning to draw," the Dormouse suddenly resumed, though in a very sleepy voice; "and they drew all manner of things—everything that ended in ION—"

"Why with ION?" said John.

"Why not?" said the March Hare, who loved these rhetorical questions as much as John disliked them.

By this time the Dormouse was nearly asleep; but on being squeezed by the Hatter it woke up again and went on, "that ends in ION, such as addition, and subtraction, and bullion, and superstition, and opposition, and resignation—did you ever see a drawing of a resignation?"

"I got the *with*drawing of a resignation once," said the March Hare, looking at the Hatter.

This piece of rudeness to the Dormouse was more than John could bear; he got up in great disgust and walked off; the Dormouse fell asleep, and the last time he saw his hosts the March Hare and the Hatter were trying to cram the Dormouse up into the Protection teapot.

"At any rate, I'l never go there again," said John, as he picked his way through Parliament Street. "It's the maddest tea-party I was ever at in my life."

Chapter VIII

"It's My Own Invention"

John walked and walked through the streets till he came to roads and at last into real country. After a while he came to a field with a large gate upon which was written "Shef Field", whilst near by was a notice saying "To the Caucus Race". He went along a little path till he came to a clump of trees, and as it was a hot day he sat down for a while and wondered if he should ever get back to his own country— for, as his friends told him, he was a great Little Englander.

At this moment his thoughts were suddenly interrupted by a loud shouting of "Ahoy! Ahoy! Check!" and a Knight, dressed in crimson armour, came swooping down upon him, brandishing a Free Food League. (John had by this time discovered that Clubs were sometimes called Leagues when they had anything to do with Sections.) Just as he reached him the horse stopped suddenly. "I've got you," the Knight cried, as he tumbled off his horse.

John wondered at this strange move, because when he saw "GORST" embroidered on the trappings he recognized the Knight as an ex-School Attendance Officer. Whilst he was wondering if it all meant he had to go to school in the Fiscal Wonderland, the Red Knight had picked himself up and got into the saddle again. "I've got—" he began again, but here another voice broke in, "Yah-yah! Yah-yah!" and John looked round to see who the new enemy might be.

This time it was the White Knight, whom John recognized as having met before on the parade ground when he was driven off the field by the mutinous loaves. He came up to John's side, exactly as the Red Knight had done, and tumbled off too, exactly in the same way. Then he got on his horse again, and the two Knights sat and glared at each other without speaking, John growing more and more bewildered all the time as to what they wanted him for and what they would do to him when they had got him.

"He's mine—you know," the Red Knight said at last.

"He was until *I* came and rescued him!" the White Knight replied.

"Well, we must fight for him, then," said the Red Knight, as he took up his helmet (which hung from his saddle and looked to be a very odd kind) and put it on.

"You will observe the Rules of Arithmetic, of course?" the Red Knight added, as he put on his helmet.

"It all depends," said the White Knight; and they began banging away at each other with so much noise that John got behind a tree so as to escape all chance of getting hit.

"These Rules seem to be very odd," said John to himself, as he looked on at the fight. "One Rule seems to be that if one Knight makes a motion the other makes an exactly contrary one: if one becomes motionless, the other does so too. And when either makes a good point, his horse stamps the ground as if he were cheering at a political meeting."

After a prodigious amount of noisy buffeting about they both became motionless, embraced each other, and then the Red Knight galloped off.

"It's My Own Invention"

"It was a glorious victory, wasn't it?" said the White Knight, as he got off his horse and came up breathing heavily.

"I don't know," said John doubtfully. "I don't want to be had by anybody. I want to be myself."

"So you will," said the White Knight, "if you come on for a bit with me. This field is where I come from, and I can show you all the paths about here."

"Thank you very much," said John. "Wouldn't you be more comfortable with your helmet off?" It was a great struggle to get it off, but John managed it at last.

"Now one can breathe more easily," said the Knight. John was much relieved at this, because he had been rather frightened at the White Knight's voice, which seemed to go right through him.

John Bull thought he had never seen such a weird-looking soldier since the Yeomanry left for South Africa. He was dressed in tinplate armour, and he had a queer little sieve fastened across his shoulders upside down. John looked at it with great curiosity.

"Oh, you're admiring my little sieve," said, or rather shouted the Knight, for he always spoke in high tones. "It's my own invention—to keep prison-made goods out. You see, I carry it upside down, so that the foreigner ca'n't get in."

"But the things can get *through*," John gently remarked. "Do you know it's full of little brushes?"

"I didn't know it," said the Knight, looking very crestfallen. "Then all these brushes must have got through! And the sieve is no good if they do that." He unfastened it as he spoke, and was just going to throw it into the ditch when a happy thought seemed to strike him, and he hung it with great care on to a tree. "I wonder if you can guess why I do that?" he said to John, who had not, however, an idea.

"In hopes that someone may take a brush—then I should show them up in the papers."

"Are these the papers you mean?" said John, pointing to the horse's shoulder, where there was a bundle of sheets with curious little red marks all over them.

"No, those are maps," said the Knight, "with all the King's dominions marked in red."

"I was wondering what the red meant," said John. "It isn't very likely, though, you'd want a map if you're only out for a ride."

"Not very likely," said the Knight, "but if the worst comes, I shouldn't like to find myself in a foreign country."

"You see," he said, after a pause, "it's as well to be provided for *everything*; that's the reason the horse has anklets round his feet."

"But what are they for?" John asked.

"To guard against dumps," the Knight replied. "It's an invention of my own."

"It's My Own Invention"

"And what's in that bag?" said John, pointing to what looked like a very heavy bag slung on to the saddle.

"That's full of 'arf-a-bricks," said the Knight.

"What are they for?" said John.

"Why, to heave at the foreigners, of course," said the Knight, much surprised at John's not knowing such a simple thing as that. "Come," he added, "I'll go with you to the end of the field."

And so they set off together, the Knight on his horse with John walking rather apprehensively at his side.

"I hope you know how to keep your hair on," said the Knight, as they went on their way.

"Oh, nothing more than usual," said John, amused at the Knight's anxiety.

"That's hardly enough," he said. "The wind's so very strong here—there are always so many people trying to raise it, you know."

"Have you invented any plan for keeping one's hair on?" John inquired.

"Not at present," said the Knight. "But I've got a plan for making it stand up on end."

"That sounds very interesting," said John. "I should like to hear about that."

"You take a leaflet, one of my own invention," said the Knight, "and read how many millions' worth of manufactured goods come in from abroad each year. Then you multiply by 20 to turn it into shillings, next you divide by 52 to reduce it to weeks, and then you divide again by 30 to reduce it to workmen. Then you think of all the workmen who haven't got the work, and of all the foreigners who have, and your hair is standing up as straight as the Queen's Westminsters. You can try it if you like. It's my own invention."

"Dear me," said John. "I had heard of that, but I thought it was Mr Chamberlain's idea."

"He got it from me," said the White Knight in a whisper (it wasn't much of a whisper, but it was the best he could do). "He gets *most* of his best ideas from me."

"It's My Own Invention"

Whosesoever idea it was, John did not think much of it, and for a few minutes they went on in silence, John every now and again stopping to help the poor Knight, who certainly was *not* a good rider.

Whenever the horse stopped (which it did very often) he fell off in front; and whenever it went on (which it always did very unexpectedly) he fell off behind. Sometimes he fell off sideways, generally on the side on which John was walking, so that John kept a good distance, though he never got out of earshot.

"I'm afraid you've not had much practice in riding," said John, anxious to make the best excuse for this on-and-off sort of performance.

The Knight looked sadly at John and said, "That's just it. Unmounted men preferred, you know, and they wouldn't let me go to the front."

John thought that if the Knight had gone he would have been unmounted, but what he said was, "It was very good of you to want to go."

"Oh, I wanted to go right enough," said the Knight. "I volunteered all over the place, but all they could be got to say was 'Thank you'."

"I'm sorry you were so disappointed," said John.

There was a short silence after this; then the Knight began again. "I'm a great hand at inventing things. Here's a thing I invented."

As he spoke he pointed to a Big Revolver.

"I invented that," he said, speaking as though he were telling a great secret, "to frighten alien immigrants from landing."

"I thought," said John Bull, "that the Big Revolver was Lord Lansdowne's idea, and that he wanted it to frighten Ambassadors with."

"He borrowed the idea from me," said the Knight. "They all get their best ideas from me," he went on, with pardonable pride.

"What's that?" said John, pointing to a weird-looking contrivance, upon the handle of which the Knight's hand rested.

"It's my own invention," said the Knight. When John looked at it it turned out to be an immense rubber stamp. It had an enormous handle, whilst on the end was this curious looking lettering—

MADE IN GERMANY *(mirrored)*

"Whenever," said the Knight, "I see anything not made in this country—apples and oysters and plums, in fact anything—I always stamp it with this,"

"You must be kept very busy," said John. "But perhaps when once they find out where the things come from, they never get any more."

A sad look came into the Knight's eyes.

"That's exactly what I had hoped would happen when I first invented it. But the disappointing thing is that they only sent for more, because, you see, when they saw 'MADE IN GERMANY', they knew where to send for them."

"Is that how it reads?" said John, who wondered what the words really were.

Here a splendid idea struck the Knight. He would stamp the top of John's hat just to show him how the stamp worked. He grasped the handle in some excitement, and instantly rolled out of the saddle and fell headlong into a deep ditch.

John ran to the side of the ditch, much frightened. He could see nothing of the Knight except the soles of his feet, but he was much relieved to hear him saying, "Yah-yah! Yah-yah!" in quite his usual tone. "I want to get it altered to 'MADE ABROAD', so that they wouldn't know where to send," he said, "but they're always too busy to get the words changed."

"How *can* you go on talking so loudly, head downwards?" said John, as he pulled him out by the feet and landed him on the bank.

The Knight looked surprised at this question. "What difference does it make where my body is?" he said. "My mind goes on working just the same. In fact, when I'm head downwards I invent more than ever.

"Now the cleverest thing I ever did," he said, when he had recovered his breath a little, "was inventing a new Tariff during the dinner-hour."

"In time to have it working by the next day?" said John. "Well, that was quick work indeed."

"Well, not the *next* day," said the Knight, considering. "No, certainly not the next *day*."

"Then I suppose it must have been the next month?"

"Well, not the *next* month," the Knight repeated as before. "Not the next *month*. In fact," he went on whispering with all his might, "I don't believe that Tariff ever was working. In fact, I don't believe that Tariff ever will be working! And yet it was a very clever Tariff to invent."

"What did you mean it to be made of?" John said, thinking it might cheer him up to talk about it.

"It *began* with ten per cent," answered the Knight, with a groan.

"That wasn't very high, I'm afraid—"

"Not very high at first," he interrupted, "but you've no idea how soon it would have got higher. And here I must leave you."

John could only look dazed; he was thinking of all the inventions—the sieve, the maps, the anklets, the 'arf-a-bricks, the revolver, the rubber stamp, the Tariff.

"You are sad," said the Knight in an anxious tone. "Let me sing you a song to comfort you."

"Is it *very* long?" John said, who was beginning to get shy of recited poems.

"It is long," said the Knight, "but it's very beautiful. The name of the song is called *Old Age Pensions*."

"Oh, that's the name of the song, is it?" John said, feeling his way.

"No, you don't understand," the Knight said. "That's what the name is called. The name really is '*The Aged, Aged Man*'."

"Well, what *is* the song?" said John, completely bewildered.

"The song," said the Knight, "really *is* '*A-Sitting on a Fence*', and the tune's my own invention."

So saying, he stopped his horse, and, having shouted "'Tention!" began beating time with one hand, and with a fond smile lighting up his curious features.

"After all, the tune *isn't* his own invention," John said to himself. "It's '*I give thee all, I can no more*'." He stood and listened very attentively.

I'll tell thee everything there is;
    It hasn't got much sense.
I saw an aged, aged man
    A-sitting on a fence.
"Who are you, aged man?" I said,
    "And why is it you wait?"
And his answer trickled through my head,
    Like water off a plate.

He saidy "I lovely orchids take
    That grow among the wheat,
They make a tasty squeezed sponge-cake,
    I sell them in the street:
I sell them unto men," he said,
    "Who want to be M.P.s,
And that's the way I beg my bread—
    A trifle, if you please."

But I was thinking of a plan
    Of dyeing butter green.
And putting on so small a tax
    That it could not be seen,
So, having no reply to give
    To what the old man said,
I cried, "Come, tell me how you live!"
    And shook him by the head.

His accents mild took up the tale;
    He said, "I go my ways,
And when I see Free Traders meet
    I set them in a blaze;
And then they talk both loud and tall,
    And say, 'The great man gains,'
Yet twopence-halfpenny is all
    They give me for my pains."

But I was thinking of a way
  On foreigners to batten,
And so contrive from day to day
  On export trade to fatten.
I shook him well from side to side,
  Until his face was blue;
"Come, tell me how you live," I cried,
  "And what it is you do."

He said, "I hunt for pickle-jars
  Among the maize so bright,
And turn them into nice pearl buttons
  In the silent night.
And these I do not sell for pence,
  Or coin of silvery hue,
But for a golden sovereign,
  And that will purchase two.

"I sometimes fish for cups of tea
  With bait my own invention;
I sometimes search at Highbury
  To find my Old Age Pension.
And that's the way (he heaved a sigh)
  By which I get my wealth;
And now since I'm so precious dry
  I'll drink your Honour's health."

I heard him then as I was trying
  To frame a method plain.
To keep the L.C.C. from buying
  Their tramline rails in Spain.
I thanked him much for telling me
  The way he got his wealth,
But chiefly for his wish that he
  Might drink my noble health.

And now if e'er by chance I stick
  My fingers in the ink,
Or when the fog's so very thick
  I cannot sleep a wink,
Or if I shout out loudly "No!"
  When only "Aye" is sense,

I weep, for it reminds me so
Of that old man with speech so slow,
Who seemed distracted with his woe
Because he did not, could not know,
Although he wandered to and fro,
And searched the country high and low,
Precisely where he ought to go
To find the Old Age Pension show—
That summer evening long ago,
  A-sitting on the fence.

As the Knight sang the last words of the hymn he turned his horse's head along the road by which they had come. "You've only a few yards to go," he said. "But you'll see me off first?" he added. "It wo'n't take me long. You'll wave your handkerchief to me when I get to that turn of the road?" It will make me feel less lonely."

"Of course I will," said John. "And thank you very much for your company—and for the song. I liked it very much."

"I hope you did," said the Knight, "but I'm dreadfully afraid you wo'n't remember it."

John was perfectly sure he wouldn't, but he thought it unnecessary to sadden the Knight by saying he wouldn't, so they shook hands, and then the Knight rode away back along the path to the Shef Field gate. As it proved, he was quite right; it did *not* take long to see him off. "There he goes," said John, "right off his head, as usual!" He went on talking to himself till the White Knight was completely out of sight; then he turned to go on his way to find to his great surprise the funniest little old gentleman sitting on what looked like an enormous mushroom.

Chapter IX

A Chanclerpillar gives Advice

The Chanclerpillar and John Bull looked at each other for some time without a word passing; at last the Chanclerpillar took the cigar out of its mouth and asked him very deliberately, "How are *you*?"

This seemed rather like a cross-examination. John replied rather shyly, "I—hardly know, sir, just at present—at least, I know how I feel myself, but everybody I meet has a different opinion as to how I feel."

"That wo'n't do, you know," said the Chanclerpillar in the judgiest of intonations. "Explain yourself."

"I ca'n't explain myself, I'm afraid, sir," said John, "because if I believe what I'm told I'm beside myself, you see."

"I don't see at all," said the Chanclerpillar, "and unless you stick to the point I shall move that you be no longer heard."

"I wish I could put it more clearly," John said; "but I'm quite as much at sea as you are, for when everybody knows how you feel better than you yourself it's dreadfully bewildering."

"It isn't," snapped out the Chanclerpillar, who seemed ready to deny any proposition.

"Well, perhaps you don't find it so now," said John, "but when you've got off that comfortable seat—you will some day, you know—"

"I sha'n't," said the Chanclerpillar. "I always feel just as well and young as ever."

"Well, perhaps," suggested John, "they're afraid to tell you how you ought to feel."

"Not a bit," said the Chanclerpillar. "But whatever they say, I just go on sitting here, making myself comfortable."

"Well, perhaps you haven't got any feelings," said John. "But all I know is it all has a very different effect upon *me*."

"You!" almost snorted the Chanclerpillar. "Who are *you*?"

A Chanclerpillar gives Advice

This seemed like getting back to just where they started. John did not like this style of cross-examining question, so, drawing himself to his full height, he said, with rather an injured air, "I think it's your turn now to answer a question. Who are *you*?"

The Chanclerpillar seemed on the point of answering with a question, but what it did say was, "I am what I have been."

John thought this so unfriendly that he turned away to go.

"Come back," shouted the Chanclerpillar. "I'm ready to give judgement."

"Yes, m'lud," said John, affected by the very legal state of the atmosphere.

"I'm a person of rank," said the Chanclerpillar.

"What rank?" said John, agreeably surprised at this communicativeness.

"Rank Protectionism," said the Chanclerpillar, with a little chuckle.

This was much more amusing, and John thought after all he might pick up something worth knowing. For some minutes the Chanclerpillar dozed on its comfortable perch, but at last it stretched its arms and said, "So you think you're changed, do you?"

"Well, I'm afraid I must be," said John, "because what so many people say must be true. I don't seem to be able to remember things, for all the history I learnt at school seems to be wrong, and I don't seem to be the same size for ten minutes together!"

"Ca'n't remember what things?" said the Chanclerpillar.

"Well, whenever I try to say, '*How doth the little busy bee*', it is always '*How doth our pushful Joey C.*'," John replied mournfully.

"Try '*You are old, Father William*'," said the Chanclerpillar. So John began:—

"You are old, Father Joseph," the young man said,
　　"Though your head doesn't show any white,
And yet you incessantly stand on your head.
　　Do you think at your age it is right?"

"In my youth," Father Joseph replied to his son,
　　"I thought it might give me a pain,
But now that I know it's so easily done,
　　Why, I do it again and again."

A Chanclerpillar gives Advice

"You are old," said the lad, as he looked at his sire,
　"Though you haven't by laughing grown fat,
Yet your wonderful somersaults keep getting higher—
　Pray, what is the inside of that?"

"In my Radical days," said the Sage, with a sneer,
　"'Take it all lying down' was my motto.
I've abandoned that now, though, for many a year,
　And in consequence, see where I've got to."

"You are old," said the lad, "and to tell you the truth,
  Your cheek grows remarkably hollow;
Yet you've eaten the speeches you made in your youth—
  Pray how do you manage the swallow?"

"Ever since," said the father, "the year '85
  I've had 'what I have said' as my diet.
Though unpleasant at first, still I've managed to thrive:
  You yourself may one day have to try it."

A Chanclerpillar gives Advice

"You are old," said the son, "one would hardly suppose
   That your I was as potent as ever,
Yet you balance statistics till nobody knows
   What they lead to—what makes you so clever?"

"I suppose it must just be a family trait,"
   Said his father, "so give yourself airs,
And maybe—who knows?—on some future fine day,
   As a peer they may kick you upstairs."

"That is not said right," said the Chanclerpillar.
"Of course it isn't," said John. "I told you I couldn't remember things."

"You are dead wrong from beginning to end," said the Chanclerpillar, as it settled itself for a short snooze.

It woke up as usual with a question.

"What size would you like to be?" it asked.

"Well, I should like to be a *little* larger, sir, if you wouldn't mind," said John, "than Mr Chamberlain makes me. Six inches is such a wretched height to be."

"It's a splendid height," said the Chanclerpillar angrily, for six inches was a good deal more than its own height.

"But I'm not used to being so small," pleaded John. "You see, it's such a sudden change, for all these years they've never left off telling me what a fine fellow I was."

"Well, you'll get used to it in time," said the Chanclerpillar; and it put the cigar back into its mouth and went on smoking again.

Just then the March Hare came bustling up as if he had something important to say and wished to say it as quickly as possible, for fear that if he didn't get it over and done with he would never get it said at all.

"Would you be so very kind, Mr Chanclerpillar," he began briskly, but that was all he ever got the chance of saying, for before he could get any farther the Chanclerpillar, in the blandest possible way, broke in with—"Don't worry, my dear Arthur," it said, with a smile. "I wouldn't for the world add to your worries by making you find someone to take my place."

"Thank you *so* much," said the March Hare meekly; but John, as he moved away, could not help thinking that he heard the March Hare (who looked very flushed and discomfited) mutter under his breath, "Bunkered again." But that may only have been his fancy, for he had not nearly got used to all the strange sights and sounds he saw and heard in the Fiscal Wonderland.

Chapter X

The Fiscal Tournament

John was only too glad when at last he got out of the field where the two Knights had fought, and once out in the road he hurried back from the country as fast as his legs would carry him.

He was very much happier when once again he was amongst streets and houses and shops, but he had not been there long before it was only too evident that something very much out of the ordinary was happening. All the people seemed to be hurrying one way, and to be wearing pictures in their buttonholes.

"Portrait of the grite man," shouted a girl whom John remembered to have seen selling flowers, as she tried to pin in John's coat a button with a picture of the Mad Hatter on it.

John had only just succeeded in warding off this attack when a second girl tried to make him buy another kind of button with what looked like two loaves on it.

John would have neither, and as he wondered what it all meant he suddenly came upon his old friend the White Rabbit, this time as a sandwichman. There he was, with a Tin Soldier, parading the streets with this curious announcement:—

John was half inclined to ask the White Rabbit what it was all about, but he remembered how excited and angry he had got when they last met, and on second thoughts decided not to.

It was very puzzling, though, not to know what was going on, and John was on the point of asking the first policeman he met, when suddenly a large Bird alighted at his side.

It was the kind that John had seen drawn in books, called the Secretary-Bird. It wore a knowing look, there were lots of quill pens stuck over its head, it carried a large notebook under one wing, and its head was hinged on like the lid of a fancy ink-bottle.

"Going to the Tournament?" said the Bird.

"Oh! It's a Tournament, is it?" said John, relieved that at all events he was beginning to find out something.

"Of course it is," said the Bird. "I thought everybody knew that."

"Well, you see," said John, "I've only just come up from the country."

"That's the worst of the provinces," said the Bird. "They're so slow."

John thought that there was such a thing as being too quick—for a motor rushed past them at the moment, going at what seemed to be about sixty miles an hour; but he did not want to offend the Bird, and he did want to find out more about the Tournament, so what he said was, "What sort of Tournament is it?"

"A Fiscal Tournament, of course," said the Bird.

"I might have known," groaned John, for when he reflected he remembered that he was in the Fiscal Wonderland.

"The Mad Hatter," continued the Bird, "has issued a challenge to all the world to meet him in single combat."

This helped John a great deal, for now he knew why the flower-girl had tried to make him buy and wear the button. He thought it would be rather fun to see the Hatter on a horse, but he was rather afraid he wouldn't be able to get in.

"All the tickets are gone," he said, "I suppose, by this time."

"Of course they are," said the Bird. At this John's face fell, but it added, "Would you like to see it?"

"Very much," said John. "You see, I once had tea with the Hatter."

"Oh! I didn't know you were a personal friend," said the Bird (John didn't know that either exactly). "In that case I think I could get you in."

"Thank you *very* much," said John, "but I'm afraid I'm giving you a lot of trouble."

"Not at all," said the Bird condescendingly. "I'm going to the Press Box to report the Tournament for my paper. There will be plenty of room for you—you're not very big, you know—and you'll be able to see and hear everything."

"If you're sure I'm not inconveniencing you," said John.

Here the Bird looked at its watch and hurriedly said, "But we mustn't waste time talking. It begins in a quarter of an hour, and we mustn't be late."

They hurried on, and as they got near where the Tournament was to be held the place had all the appearance of a huge fair. Only those who had tickets could get in to the Tournament, but there were tens of thousands of people, nearly all wearing buttons, who had come out to cheer the various champions as they made their way to the place of combat. All those who wore Hatter buttons were made to keep on one side of the road, and all with loaf buttons on the other. On the latter side there were great booths labelled "Free Trade Union" and "Unionist Free Food League". At first John thought this meant that you could have a meal for nothing, but one of the attendants at the booth explained that this was not so, and all John got was a handful of leaflets. Across the way all the banners had the word "Consistent" on them. Over the booth labelled "Imperial Tariff Committee", for instance, a flag fluttered "Consistent, Birmingham". Another immense booth was called "Tariff Reform League", and here there were orators standing on stumps of trees, each with a crowd around him.

"I suppose we haven't time," said John, "to hear what they are saying."

"If you're very quick of hearing, we have," said the Bird. "Besides," it added, "it may be good copy."

This was quite unintelligible to John, but he didn't mind so long as he could listen to what was said. This is what the orator was saying:—

> 'Tis the Voice of the Trader: I heard him declare,
> "They have done me quite brown and it's beastly unfair."
> Like a crocodile sobbing so he crieth sore
> Of the boots and the buttons he makes now no more.
> When the orders are thick he will hardly say thankee,
> And will talk in contemptuous tones of the Yankee;
> But when the wind changes and tariffs abound,
> His voice has a timid and tremulous sound.

"I wish everything wasn't so like and yet so different," said John, who felt certain that he knew the poem.

"Oh! If you're going to talk," said the Bird—so John said no more, and the orator on the stump proceeded:—

> I passed by his factory and marked with my eye,
> How two Eagles were sticking their claws in his pie;
> The German got crumbs as his share of the treat,
> While the Yankee just collared a second-hand fleet.
> When the Lion had finished the pie, with a frown
> He settled himself for a sleep, lying down,
> While the Hatter, who used an enormous long spoon,
> Stirred him up—

He had got thus far when a bell sounded.

"The saddling bell," said the Bird, and off he started, John hurrying after him.

The Bird evidently represented some important paper, for after it had whispered something to the doorkeeper John was allowed to enter, though he had no ticket. In another minute the Bird and John were sitting in the front row of an enclosure labelled "PRESS BOX". At first John felt rather shy at being with so many birds, but that soon wore off, and he found himself thinking how lucky he was to have such a good place where he could see so well.

What he saw was a large open space of turf, with barriers on either side. Inside the barriers were men and women standing, packed like herrings in a barrel, whilst at the back of the crowds were huge stands, very much like those John remembered having seen at Epsom and Newmarket in his own country.

Here, too, the spectators took different sides according to the side they took, and there were lots of boxes, each having a label on it. On the Hatter's side, for instance, the "TREASURY BOX" contained the March Hare, and a little boy, the very image of the Hatter. John felt sure this must be the Hatter's son, and sure enough, when later on the fighting began, the little fellow kept clapping his little hands and saying, "Go it, father; I do so admire you."

Another box on the same side was called the "LARGE TYPE BOX". This was so puzzling that John ventured to ask the Bird for an explanation.

"The people in that box," said the Bird, "are the people who, when they write to the *Times*, have their letters printed in large type. That" (and as he spoke he pointed with his pen) "is Mr Benjamin Kidd." He named several others, but what interested John most was to see a bird in this box.

"But who's the bird?" said John.

"That's a great secret," said the Bird, "but I don't mind telling you if you promise to keep the secret. That's 'Tariff Reformer'."

On the side of those who were against the Hatter there were boxes labelled "PROFESSORS' BOX" (in which sat fourteen very learned-looking gentlemen, all dressed in cap and gown, with a fifteenth squeezed in at the back, standing) and "EX-CHANCELLORS' BOX". There were four people in this second box, all of great experience. One of them, later on, actually fought the Hatter, and two others made it very clear that they agreed with him in doing so. But the fourth kept trying not to be seen, and whenever he did catch sight of the March Hare he always kissed his hand to him.

One other box interested John exceedingly. It was labelled the "BAD OLD TIMES BOX", and was full of very old men and women, nearly all of them agricultural labourers in smock frocks, and their womenfolk. The Bird explained to John that these had come from all parts of the country, and were those who remembered the time before the tax was taken off corn, nearly sixty years ago.

By the time John had been able to notice all this another bell rang, and as soon as it finished clanging the White Rabbit rode into the centre of the arena on an exceedingly aged Cow.

(The Bird told John that the Cow was such a favourite of the Rabbit's that he always rode it in preference to a Horse. In fact, many people declared that he had ridden it nearly to death.)

The Rabbit rang a large bell and shouted "Silence for the Great Man!" three times.

As he ended in rode the Hatter. He was received with great cheering by his own side, many of whom (as John now noticed) wore mail and spoke at express rate. The Hatter was mounted on a spirited but rather screwy horse, and rode slowly once round the ring, after which he flung down the gage (which turned out to be a little loaf) and rode back to his tent to get his armour.

"Who dares," shouted the Rabbit (it wasn't much of a shout, but it could be heard by everybody), "to oppose our Joe?"

"I do," said a Knight called Asquith, who rode into the ring.

"Let the champion appear," said the Rabbit.

The Hatter, now fully clad in his armour, galloped in, but when he saw who his opponent was gave a snort of contempt.

"Only a lawyer!" he shouted out, and with that they fell to. It was quite a short encounter. The Hatter kept shifting his ground, but once the lawyer Knight could get at him he had no difficulty in unhorsing him.

There was great cheering from the Hatter's opponents, but he wasn't in the least abashed. "I did come off well that time, didn't I?" he said to his supporters, as he rode back to his tent, at which they cheered with almost uncontrollable enthusiasm.

"Who dares to oppose our Joe?" the challenge rang out again—as much, that is to say, as the Rabbit's voice could make it ring.

This time it was a Knight named Goschen—one of the four whom John had seen in the ex-Chancellors' Box.

The Hatter rode up, but in quite a different suit of armour, for his first suit had been smashed to little bits in his first combat.

"Only a skeleton!" was his genial comment this time as the two combatants fell to. The result was precisely the same. The Skeleton Knight, though a veteran, showed such skill and deftness in conflict that the Hatter in a very short time was on the ground for a second time. He took it just as coolly, saying to his crowd, precisely as on the first occasion, "I did come off well that time, didn't I?" the crowd cheering him for all the world just as if he had won.

A third time the challenge rang forth, and this time in the challenger John recognized Twee-C.-B. When the Hatter saw who it was he rode back to his tent, and when he came out it was seen that he was wearing a feather in his cap.

Twee-C.-B. looked such a genial warrior that John was amazed to see the Hatter grow white with anger.

"Only a Little Englander!" the Hatter shouted at the top of his voice.

"Well, let's see which is the better man," sang out A Voice.

This led to great cheering and counter-cheering. The two Knights were at it before the echoes had died away, but the result was never in doubt. The Hatter, despite an entirely different set of argumentative armour, was easily floored. Even he seemed rather crestfallen, but he made his customary remark and it got the customary cheer.

As John felt certain would be the case, the next champion to enter the lists was Tweedle-R.

"What a lot better he looks since he came out of his furrow!" said the Bird.

"His furrow?" repeated John, not understanding in the least.

"Yes," said the Bird. "Some time ago he and Twee-C.-B. had a quarrel, and the end of it was that Tweedle-R. went off and lived in a Lonely Furrow."

"It sounds as if he had been ploughed," said John.

"I'm not sure that he hadn't," said the Bird. "He would keep on examining himself, you know."

There was no time to pursue the topic further, because by this time the Knights were ready for the fray. Tweedle-R. was beautifully arrayed in Imperialistic armour, whilst this time the Hatter had a wonderful suit composed of nothing but pearl buttons, all specially made (so the rumour ran in the crowd) at Birmingham by the few remaining survivors of that decayed industry.

"Tinplates and personalities, indeed," was the Hatter's polite greeting this time. The fight was a very graceful one. Tweedle-R. did not seem to exert himself, but in the most felicitous way possible got at the Great Man, whose supporters were growing visibly anxious. Nor was that anxiety lessened when in another moment he was sprawling on the turf.

"Are you going to take it lying down?" said A Voice.

There was a great shout of laughter, which completely drowned what the Hatter said to his side of the arena, though as they cheered it was probably the same old shibboleth.

In the next and (as it proved) the last of these single combats the Hatter's opponent was a Knight named Lord George. As he rode into the arena a shout of mocking welcome greeted him from the Hatter's supporters. "Well, he must fancy himself"; "Cheek I call it"; "He *will* get it"—these were some of the cries which showed how certain they made the Hatter would have an easy victory.

Certainly he did not *look* a very redoubtable adversary, and even amongst the Hatter's opponents there was a shaking of heads as if they rather thought that this time the Hatter might not come out second best.

The prospect of a more equal encounter intensified the excitement, and if pins ever made a noise when they drop on turf, you might have heard one drop as the two—the Hatter and Lord George—sat and glared at one another.

"Now we sha'n't be long," said the Hatter, and he was quite right. For of all the champions none acquitted himself more redoubtably than did Lord George. "Well, I *am* surprised"; "Never knew it was in him"; "That's the way to take care of your friends"—these were some of the delighted greetings of the crowd as they saw the Hatter get perhaps the most sorry beating he had had. The White Rabbit had to go and help him on to his horse, and all he could say as he rode to his tent was, "I came off better than ever *that* time,"

There were lots of other Knights ready to fight the Hatter, but it was now announced that there would be no more single combats, but that there would be a general encounter between a dozen champions on either side. By this time it was getting dark, and John looked up to find the names of the warriors flashed on to a screen.

This is what he read:—

THE HATTER'S PROPOSALS
GENERAL MÊLÉE

Pro.	Con.
The Mad Hatter.	⎰ Tweedle-R.
The White Knight.	⎱ Twee-C.-B.
The Chanclerpillar.	The Dormouse.
The Chaplin.	The Asquith Knight.
The White Rabbit.	Lord George.
The Tin Soldier.	The Skeleton Knight.
Sherlock Holmes.	The Knight of Malwood.
Dumpy Jim Lowther.	The Ritchie Knight.
The *Daily Mail*.	Sunny Jim (of Hereford).
The *Daily Express*.	The Grey Knight.
The Editor of *The Times*.	The Fowler.
Mr Benjamin Kidd.	St Augustine Birrell.

John recognized a good many old friends, as well as some whom he had seen for the first time fighting that day. The rest were explained to him by the Bird. Sherlock Holmes was fighting for the Hatter because nobody else had even a chance (let alone an even chance) of discovering who was to benefit by his proposals. Dumpy Jim was a bosom friend of the Chaplin's; they had hunted in couples all their life. The *Daily Mail* and *Daily Express* were paper Knights who fought because they were advised that it was good for their circulation. The editor of *The Times* thought the Hatter's plan could not fail to make people want to consult the *Encyclopædia Britannica* to try to discover (if possible) its meaning. Mr Benjamin Kidd was in the Hatter's dozen because he was such a staunch Liberal.

On the other side, of those whom John did not know, the Knight of Malwood was a veteran Knight who never lingered by his fireside in the New Forest when a blow could be struck for Free Trade. The Ritchie Knight John recognized at once as the man who had driven the Hatter mad—he had seen him, too, in the ex-Chancellors' Box. Sunny Jim (of Hereford) was another veteran who was always ready for a fight against any sort of corruption. The Grey Knight looked very young, but had already won renown by his skill in tackling men as well as fishes. The Fowler came from the Hatter's country, but was quite sure that *this* time he really *was* mad. St Augustine Birrell was a Knight who, though he thought the pen mightier

than the sword, knew right well how to wield both to good purpose.

By the time the Bird had given John all this information, and answered Johns numerous questions, the fight was in full swing. There is no need to describe it, as it was only a repetition on a larger scale of all the single combats that had preceded it. Even the Dormouse, who was asleep during the first few minutes, woke up and got in a number of astonishingly straight blows, most of them at the Hatter himself. The *Mail* and *Express* threw any amount of ink in the hope that some of it would stick, but the crowd easily saw through such peculiar tactics. Dumpy Jim was no match for Sunny Jim, though they were both first-class fighting men. As the fight proceeded the Hatter got madder and madder, and John was wondering what would happen to him and to the White Rabbit, who wept bitterly, when gradually the immense cloud of dust kicked up in the course of the controversy entirely blotted out the fight from his view.

"I'm off," said the Bird. "I'm going to get back and write it all up for my paper."

"Write it all down, I suppose you mean," said John; but the Bird was in no mood for more explanations, and hurried on without answering.

"Thank you *so* much for your kindness; I shall *never* forget it," said John; but the Bird was out of sight, and John could see nothing, whilst all he could hear was shouts in the distance of "The trial's beginning."

"Come on," said the Pig, against whom John suddenly stumbled. The Pig caught hold of John by the hand, greatly to his relief, for he began to be afraid that this time he really was lost.

"What trial is it?" said John as clearly as he could between his breaths as they ran; but the Pig only said, "Forward," singing as he went (it was wonderful how he managed to have so much breath, for he was as fat as could be):—

Ma—aize of the mo—mo—morning,
  Beautiful, beautiful maize!

CHAPTER XI

Who Stole the Loaves?

The King and Queen of Spades (who looked exactly like a workman and his wife in John Bull's own country) were seated on the throne when they arrived, with a great crowd assembled in court—all sorts of weird creatures, as well as the whole pack of cards; the Mad Hatter (who turned out to be the Knave of Spades) was standing before them, with two young-looking soldiers on each side to guard him; and near the King was the White Rabbit, with a trumpet (his own) in one hand and a large roll in the other. In the very middle of the court was a table, with a large number of loaves upon it; it made John quite hungry to look at them.

John had often been in a court of justice before, but never in one quite like this. The twelve jurors, all of them registered electors, were all writing very busily on their slates (some of them very dirty ones). "What are they all doing?" John whispered to the Pig. "They ca'n't want to write anything down yet before the trial's begun."

"They're putting down their politics," the Pig whispered in reply, "for fear they should forget what they are before the end of the trial."

"Free and independent, indeed," John said in a loud, angry voice, but he stopped guiltily, for the White Rabbit cried out, "Silence in the court!" and the King put on his spectacles and looked anxiously round to see who was daring to talk.

John could see quite well that all the jurors were writing down "Free and independent" on their slates, and some of them had heard so much talk about different sorts of trade that they actually didn't know how to spell "free" and wrote down "fair". "A nice muddle and mess their slates will be in before the trial's over," thought John.

"Herald, read the accusation," said the King solemnly.

The White Rabbit took up his trumpet and tried to blow it. At first he could not get any sound out of it.

At last, however, by a great effort there came a ghostlike blast, but to the great amazement of the Court it was only

"*Three Acres and a Cow.*"

The Mad Hatter looked madder than ever at this, and the White Rabbit tremblingly began to explain.

"If you please, your Majesty," he said, "my horn has been frozen for nearly twenty years, and now that it is thawed the old words have to come out first."

"Where was the horn made?" said the King.

"In Birming—" but before he had time to finish the word the Queen interrupted him by saying, "It's always the way with them Brummagem things."

The White Rabbit was so flurried and flustered that everybody saw he couldn't go on being Herald, so the King directed the Tin Soldier to take his place.

The new Herald gave three long, low whistles, and then proceeded to unroll the scroll, which proved to be an enormous envelope bearing this curious inscription:—

TRADE AND THE EMPIRE.

If you want to know what the Knave of Spades has done read the enclosed.

"CONSISTENT BIRMINGHAM."   MADE IN GERMANY.

Having opened it, he unrolled the leaflet which he found inside, and read as follows:—

> *The Queen of Spades, she baked some loaves*
> *All on her washing day;*
> *The Knave of Spades, he stole those loaves*
> *And took them quite away!*

"Consider your verdict," said the Hatter, as soon as he heard this read out.

"Not yet," said the King. "There's a great deal to come before that.

"Call the prisoner," said the King. And the Tin Soldier whistled three times and called out, "The prisoner."

This procedure puzzled John very much until one of the court cards explained that in the Fiscal Wonderland the defence always came before the prosecution, and that prisoners were allowed to give evidence themselves, as, indeed, John remembered, they now do in his own country.

The Hatter came into the witness-box with a subscription list in one hand and a leaflet in the other. "I beg pardon, your Majesty," he began, "for bringing these here, but I hadn't quite finished my Committee meeting when I was arrested and brought here."

"You ought to have finished," said the King. "When did you begin?"

The Hatter looked at the March Hare, who was in court sitting arm in arm with the Dormouse. "Fourteenth of May, I *think* it was," he said.

"Fifteenth," said the March Hare.

"I read about it on the sixteenth," added the Dormouse.

"Write that down," said the King to the jury, and the jury at once wrote down all these dates on their slates, and then added them up in quinquennial periods and set out the result in imports and exports.

"Where *did* you get that hat?" the King said to the Hatter, in a peculiar sing-song voice, as if it were part of a tune.

"It came from abroad," said the Hatter.

"*Dumped!*" the King exclaimed, turning to the jury, who instantly wrote down the word, though they hadn't an idea what it meant.

"I bought the hat," added the Hatter, by way of explanation, "in my free-trading days. I haven't wanted a new one since."

Here, since the question was one of hats, the Queen seemed very interested, and stared hard at the Hatter, who turned pale and fidgeted.

"Give your evidence," said the King, "and don't shuffle about so much, or I'll have you exported on the spot."

This seemed to disconcert the witness a good deal; he kept shifting from one foot to the other, and in his confusion made a lot of corrections in the subscription list, instead of the leaflet.

Just at this moment John discovered that he was growing large again. At first he thought of leaving the court, but on second thoughts decided to see the trial through, as long as there was room in the court.

"I wish you wouldn't squeeze so," said the Dormouse, who was sitting next to him. "I can hardly sleep a wink."

"I ca'n't help it," said John. "I'm growing."

"You've no right to grow," said the Hatter, who overheard the conversation. (He wasn't a very polite Hatter.) "I've told everybody you're in a decline."

"Don't talk nonsense," said John, annoyed at being lectured by the prisoner.

"It's no sense the way you're squeezing *me*," said the Dormouse, as he got up and chose a fresh seat as far away as he could from John.

All this time the Queen had never left off staring at the Hatter, and now she said all at once to one of the whips, "Bring me a list of the members of the last Liberal Government," on which the Hatter trembled so that he almost turned his coat.

"Give your evidence," the King repeated angrily, "or I'll have you exported, whether you're a Privy Councillor or not."

"I'm a patriotic man, your Majesty," the Hatter began in an assertive voice, "and I hadn't started my Committee—not above Austen and Jesse—and what with the Education Act working so thin—and the War Commission coming it so thick—and the cristling of the sea—"

"The cristling of the *what*?" said the King.

"I begin with a C," the Hatter replied.

"Of course cristling begins with a C," said the King sharply. "But this isn't a spelling bee, sir! Go on!"

"I'm a patriotic man," the Hatter went on, "and most things crystalled after that—and the March Hare quite agreed—"

"I didn't," the March Hare interrupted in a great hurry.

"You did," said the Hatter.

"I mean, I did," said the March Hare, who seemed afraid of disagreeing with the Hatter.

"He admits it," said the King to the jury. "Be sure you put that down."

"After that," the Hatter went on, "all the rest went off to the inquest—"

"But what did you do?" said one of the jury.

"Oh, I began to write leaflets," said the Hatter, and proceeded to hand one to each of the jury. Oddly enough, the Tin Soldier actually helped him to do it until this skilful game was stopped by the King, in a very stern voice, ordering all the leaflets to be impounded.

That was a very hard word, which made John Bull wonder what would happen, but all that did happen was that the leaflets were collected and given to the King and Queen, who immediately began to study them intently.

One that was headed "The Cost of Living" seemed to excite the Queen very much, and at last, when she had read it through, she said, "You'd soon know about the cost of living if you had to feed as many mouths as I have."

Here a dozen or so of children who were in court cheered heartily, they were so excited at hearing their mother make such a long speech in public.

"The figures are all wrong," said the King sternly.

"Of course they are," said the Hatter, "but then, you see, the figures are only illustrations. I do not pretend that they are proofs; the proofs will be found in the argument, and not in the figures. But I use figures as illustrations to show what the argument is."

The Tin Soldier and the White Rabbit (who had crept back into court) made an attempt at a cheer, but it was a very feeble one.

What the King said was, "If that's all you can say, you may stand down."

"I ca'n't go no lower," said the Hatter. "I've played it pretty low down as it is already."

"Then you must take it lying down," said the King, with a chuckle, as if by saying that he in some way scored off the prisoner.

As it was, the Hatter was put back into the dock, where he was again taken charge of by the two soldiers (whose names were Winston and Hugh) after an unsuccessful attempt had been made to rescue the Hatter by some ill-favoured loafers, who shouted all the time. "Shall the Radicals be allowed to attack our Joe?"

"Call the next witness," said the King.

John watched the Tin Soldier as he fumbled over the list, feeling very interested to know who the next witness would be—"for they haven't made much of a defence yet," he said to himself. Great was his surprise when the Tin Soldier looked at him and said, with an air of immense authority, "John Bull!"

CHAPTER XII

John Bull's Evidence

"Here," said John, quite forgetting how much bigger than the rest he was, and he jumped up in such a hurry that he completely upset the jury-box. Over they went into the court, slates and all, and they had to be collected and put back into their places, though they none of them got their own slates again, with the result that they got more and more muddled as the trial proceeded.

"What do you know about this business?" the King said to John.

"Everything," said John.

"Everything imaginable?" said the King.

"Everything real *and* imaginable," said John.

"That's not true," said the March Hare from the body of the court.

This caused a great commotion, but when the Tin Soldier had got some sort of order again the March Hare added, "He hasn't seen my second pamphlet."

"That's quite true, your Majesty," said John, who had grown wonderfully self-possessed, "but I know what's in it."

The March Hare hurriedly felt his pocket.

"It's only one of the Hatter's leaflets," said John, "with all the short words taken out and long ones put in in their place."

This led to a regular scene. A Wicket-keeper, saying that he's known the March Hare all his life and had perfect faith in his honour, tried to get at John Bull, and nearly lost his own seat in consequence. Almost everybody shouted something or other except the March Hare, who, looking very flushed, kept absolutely silent. It was whispered in court that this was because he had nothing to say.

The King thought the only thing to do was to finish the trial as quickly as possible. "Consider your verdict," he said to the jury in a low, trembling voice.

"Please your Majesty," said the Tin Soldier, "there's a witness waiting outside who's dreadfully anxious to give evidence."

"Let him appear," said the King, and all the Court eagerly awaited the appearance of this new witness.

The door opened, and then, to the amazement of everybody,

the court waiters brought in a large dish with an enormous Leg of Mutton on it, and placed it on top of the witness-box.

Without waiting to be introduced, the Leg of Mutton got up and bowed to the King and Queen, but before it had time to say anything a great shout of laughter went up as everybody saw who it was.

"Take it away," said the King, and away it was

carried, muttering as it went something about the cold shoulder.

"Consider your verdict," said the King once again.

"Please your Majesty," said the Tin Soldier, "this paper has just been picked up."

"Another leaflet," said the Queen.

"I haven't opened it yet," said the Tin Soldier, "but it seems to be a letter in the prisoner's writing."

"Who is it directed to?" said one of the jurymen.

"It hasn't got any direction," said the Tin Soldier, "In fact, it isn't a letter; its a set of verses."

"And not in the Hatter's handwriting?" said the King.

"No," said the Tin Soldier, "and I know his handwriting well."

"He must have forced somebody else's hand," said the King.

"Please your Majesty," said the Hatter, "you ca'n't prove I wrote the verses. There's no reason for what I did, and there ca'n't be any rhyme either."

The Tin Soldier and the White Rabbit clapped their hands vigorously at this clever repartee, but the Queen frowned and said, "I think that proves his guilt."

"Nothing of the kind," said the Hatter jauntily.

"Read the verses," said the King.

These were the verses which the Tin Soldier read:—

> *They told me when I made the stir,*
>   *You called and found him in;*
> *He gave me a good character,*
>   *But said I should not win.*
>
> *They wondered all if I had gone*
>   *(We knew it to be true);*
> *If I should push the matter on,*
>   *What would become of you?*

They hit me one, I hit them two,
    You gave them three or more;
They all returned from me to you,
    Though most were mine before.

If you and I should chance to be
    Involved by this affair,
Just trust to me to set you free
    Exactly as we were.

My notion was that he had been
    (Before I had this fit)
The obstacle that came between
    You and ourselves and it.

Don't let them know you like me best,
    For this must ever be
A secret kept from all the rest
    Between yourself and me.

"That's the most damning piece of evidence we've heard yet," said the King, "so now let the jury—"

"If any one of them," said the Hatter, growing desperate, "can explain it, I pledge myself that his cost of living shall never be increased. In fact" (and here he burst into song):—

    "*I pledge my word the Empire needs Protection;*
        I pledge my word that through Protection we will gain;
    I pledge my word that this will benefit the nation—
        These are the words of Joseph Chamberlain.

I assert that there isn't an atom of meaning in it."

The jury all wrote down on each other's slate: "*He* asserts there isn't an atom of meaning in it."

"If there's no meaning in it," said the King, "that would save a world of trouble. And yet I don't know," he went on, holding up the verses to the light. "I seem to see some meaning in them after all—*'said I should not win'*. You ca'n't win, can you?" he added, turning to the Hatter.

The Hatter shook his head despairingly. "I always say I can, but do I look like it?" he said. (Which he certainly did *not*, being entirely clad in fustian.)

"All right so far," said the King, and he went on muttering through the verses: "'*If I should push the matter on*'—that looks as if it had something to do with pushfulness. '*They hit me one, I hit them two*'—now, that must mean something you did."

"Yes," said the Dormouse in a rare interval of wakefulness, "that's how he always used to translate *'Bis dat qui cito dat'*."

"Quite so," said the King, delighted to have his authority supported from such a very unexpected quarter. "Let the jury consider their verdict."

"No, no!" shrieked the Hatter, growing madder than ever. "Policy first, inquiry afterwards."

"Stuff and nonsense!" said John. "The idea of make-believing to inquire into what you know beforehand!"

"Hold your tongue!" said the Hatter.

"I wo'n't!" said John Bull.

"Off with his head!" said the Hatter.

"Who cares for you?" said John Bull. "Why, you're nothing but a Protectionist."

"Take him away," said the King and Queen together in stern voices, and the two soldiers at once led off the Mad Hatter to prison.

When he had gone the Tin Soldier and the White Rabbit made a dash at John. He tried to beat them off, and found himself in his armchair with Britannia beside him trying to keep away the flies that buzzed around him.

"Wake up, John, dear," said Britannia.

"All right, Your Royal Highness," said John Bull, only half awake.

"Royal Highness, indeed!" said Britannia. "You *have* grown polite in your sleep."

"Oh! I've had such a real sort of adventure," said John, seeing it was only Britannia, and he told her all he could remember of his doings in the Fiscal Wonderland.

When he had finished his wife kissed him, and said, "It was a bad dream, dear, certainly; you've only yourself to thank if it ever does come true. But now come and have your dinner; it's getting late."

So John went and dined wisely and well (but not too well), thinking whilst he enjoyed his dinner how fortunate he was to have such good food, such cheap food, and such plenty of it.

Also available from Evertype

Alice's Adventures in Wonderland, 2008

Through the Looking-Glass and What Alice Found There
2009

Wonderland Revisited and the Games Alice Played There
by Keith Sheppard, 2009

A New Alice in the Old Wonderland
by Anna Matlack Richards, 2009

New Adventures of Alice
by John Rae, 2010

Alice's Adventures under Ground, 2009

The Nursery "Alice", 2010

The Hunting of the Snark, 2010

Alice's Adventures in Wonderland,
Retold in words of one Syllable by Mrs J. C. Gorham, 2010

Clara in Blunderland, by Caroline Lewis, 2010

Lost in Blunderland: The further adventures of Clara
by Caroline Lewis, 2010

The Westminster Alice, by H. H. Munro (Saki), 2010

Alice in Blunderland, by John Kendrick Bangs, 2010

Eachtraí Eilíse i dTír na nIontas
Alice in Irish, 2007

Lastall den Scáthán agus a bhFuair Eilís Ann Roimpi
Looking-Glass in Irish, 2009

Alys in Pow an Anethow
Alice in Cornish, 2009

La Aventuroj de Alicio en Mirlando
Alice in Esperanto, 2009

Les Aventures d'Alice au pays des merveilles
Alice in French, 2010

Alice's Abenteuer im Wunderland
Alice in German, 2010

Le Avventure di Alice nel Paese delle Meraviglie
Alice in Italian, 2010

Contoyrtyssyn Ealish ayns Cheer ny Yindyssyn
Alice in Manx, 2010

Alice's Äventyr i Sagolandet
Alice in Swedish, 2010

Anturiaethau Alys yng Ngwlad Hud
Alice in Welsh, 2010

www.ingramcontent.com/pod-product-compliance
Lightning Source LLC
Chambersburg PA
CBHW030000050426
42451CB00006B/73